PagePlus X4
Resource Guide

Credits

This Resource Guide, and the software described in it, is furnished under an end user License Agreement, which is included with the product. The agreement specifies the permitted and prohibited uses.

Portions images © 1997-2002 Nova Development Corporation; © 1995 Expressions Computer Software; © 1996-98 CreatiCom, In.; 1996 Cliptoart; © 1997 Multimedia Agency Corporation; © 1997-98 Seattle Support Group. Rights of all parties reserved.

Digital Images ©2008 Hemera Technologies Inc. All Rights Reserved.

Digital Images ©2008 Jupiterimages Corporation, All Rights Reserved.

Digital Images ©2008 Jupiterimages France SAS, All Rights Reserved.

Bitstream Font content © 1981-2005 Bitstream Inc. All rights reserved.

Panose Typeface Matching System ©1991, 1992, 1995-97 Hewlett-Packard Corporation.

Portions graphics import/export technology © AccuSoft Corp. & Eastman Kodak Company & LEAD Technologies, Inc.

THE PROXIMITY HYPHENATION SYSTEM © 1989 Proximity Technology Inc. All rights reserved.

THE PROXIMITY/COLLINS DATABASE © 1990 William Collins Sons & Co. Ltd.; © 1990 Proximity Technology Inc. All rights reserved.

THE PROXIMITY/MERRIAM-WEBSTER DATABASEÒ © 1990 Merriam-Webster Inc.; © 1990 Proximity Technology Inc. All rights reserved.

The Sentry Spelling-Checker Engine © 2000 Wintertree Software Inc.

The ThesDB Thesaurus Engine © 1993-97 Wintertree Software Inc.

WGrammar Grammar-Checker Engine © 1998 Wintertree Software Inc.

Extensible Metadata Platform (XMP) Copyright © 2006 Adobe Systems Incorporated. All rights reserved.

ICC Colour Profiles © 2006 Adobe Systems Incorporated. All rights reserved.

PANTONE® Colours displayed in the software application or in the user documentation may not match PANTONE-identified standards. Consult current PANTONE Colour Publications for accurate colour. PANTONE® and other Pantone, Inc. trademarks are the property of Pantone, Inc. ©Pantone, Inc., 2001

Pantone, Inc. is the copyright owner of colour data and/or software which are licensed to Serif (Europe) Ltd. to distribute for use only in combination with PagePlus. PANTONE Colour Data and/or Software shall not be copied onto another disk or into memory unless as part of the execution of PagePlus.

FontForge © 2000,2001,2002,2003,2004,2005,2006,2007,2008 by George Williams.

Portions of this software are copyright © 2008 The FreeType Project (www.freetype.org). All rights reserved.

ODF Translator © 2006-2008, Clever Age, DIaLOGIKa, Sonata Software Ltd. All rights reserved.

Office Binary Translator to OpenXML Copyright © 2008-2009, DIaLOGIKa All rights reserved.

Clipart samples from Serif ArtPacks © Serif (Europe) Ltd. & Paul Harris

TrueType font samples from Serif FontPacks © Serif (Europe) Ltd.

PagePlus is a registered trademark of Serif (Europe) Ltd.

Microsoft, Windows, and the Windows logo are registered trademarks of Microsoft Corporation. All other trademarks acknowledged.

© 2009 Serif (Europe) Ltd. All rights reserved. No part of this Resource Guide may be reproduced in any form without the express written permission of Serif (Europe) Ltd.

Serif PagePlus X4 © 2009 Serif (Europe) Ltd.

How to contact us

Contacting Serif technical support

Our support mission is to provide fast, friendly technical advice and support from a team of on-call experts. Technical support is provided from our web support page, and useful information can be obtained via our web-based forums (see below). There are no pricing policies after the 30 day money back guarantee period.

UK/International/
US Technical Support: http://www.serif.com/support

Additional Serif contact information

Web:

Serif Website: http://www.serif.com

Forums: http://www.serif.com/forums.asp

Main office (UK, Europe):

The Software Centre, PO Box 2000, Nottingham, NG11 7GW, UK

Main: (0115) 914 2000

Registration (UK only):   (0800) 376 1989

Sales (UK only):   (0800) 376 7070

Customer Service
(UK/International):   http://www.serif.com/support

General Fax: (0115) 914 2020

North American office (US, Canada):

The Software Center, 13 Columbia Drive, Suite 5, Amherst NH 03031, USA

Main: (603) 889-8650

Registration: (800) 794-6876

Sales: (800) 55-SERIF or 557-3743

Customer Service: http://www.serif.com/support

General Fax: (603) 889-1127

International enquiries:

Please contact our main office.

Contents

Introduction

Welcome to the PagePlus X4 Resource Guide! Whether you are new to PagePlus or a seasoned desktop publisher, this guide offers content to help you get the best out of PagePlus.

From a range of illustrated tutorials to get you started or help you accomplish a complex project, to full-colour previews of the design packs, theme layouts, and logo templates, the Resource Guide is something you'll return to time and time again.

The Resource Guide is organized into the following chapters:

- **Chapter 1: Tutorials**
  Illustrated, step-by-step training covering the basics of PagePlus and desktop publishing, along with a range of design-focused exercises and more challenging projects.

- **Chapter 2: Design Packs**
  A reference gallery of the design pack template sets available on the PagePlus X4 Program CD and its accompanying Resource DVD.

- **Chapter 3: Theme Layouts**
  Full-colour page previews of the theme layout sets included on the PagePlus X4 Program CD.

- **Chapter 4: LogoStudio & Logo Templates:**
  Previews of the customizable logo templates included with PagePlus, and instructions on how to add them to your publications.

How the Resource Guide was made

The Resource Guide was created and output using PagePlus, employing many powerful PagePlus features. These include:

- **BookPlus** to unify separate publications with a common page numbering system.

- **Mail and Photo Merge with Repeating Areas** to automatically create pages with picture content based on a folder of images.

- **Find and Replace** functionality to apply text styles consistently and quickly throughout the text.

The content was incorporated into a PagePlus book comprised of multiple publication chapters. The book was then published as a press-ready PDF—accurately maintaining all text, fonts, images, and native colouring—in a CMYK colour format suitable for professional printing.

Tutorials

1

Introduction

These tutorials were designed to help you get the most out of the program. They are grouped into three categories—**Basics**, **Design**, and **Projects**—so whatever your level of expertise, you're sure to find something that interests you.

To access files needed by the tutorials, browse to the **...\Workspace** folder in your PagePlus installation directory.

In a standard installation, you'll find this in the following location:

C:\Program Files\Serif\PagePlus\X4\Tutorials

We hope you enjoy working through these exercises.

> The tutorials are also presented as PDF files, which you can print out or view on screen.
>
> If viewing on screen, you can quickly switch between PagePlus and the tutorial document by pressing the **Alt + Tab** keys.

Basics

Aimed at the new user, these exercises introduce you to PagePlus and help you get to grips with the more common desktop publishing tools and techniques.

Quick Start

Create professional-looking documents quickly and easily. Start with a theme layout template, add your own images and text, and change your colour scheme.

In this tutorial, we'll show you how to:

- Open a **Theme Layout** template.
- Update **User Details**.
- Edit and format text.
- Add and adjust images.
- Change your colour scheme.

Quick Start

PagePlus provides a wide range of professionally designed theme layouts, which you can use as starting points for your own publications, adding your own pictures and text.

In this tutorial, we'll show you just how easy it is to create an eye-catching, professional-looking document using a theme layout template.

To open a theme layout

1   On the **File** menu, click **New > New from Startup Wizard**.

2   Click **Use Design Template**.

3   In the dialog:

- Click to expand **Theme Layouts** and then click the **Spiro** category.

- In the centre pane, click to select the **Newsletter** thumbnail.

- In the **Pages** pane, click the check boxes to select the pages that you want to use in your publication—we selected pages 1 and 2.

- In the drop-down list, you can choose from three specially designed schemes, or any of the colour schemes included with PagePlus. We selected **Scheme 1**.

- Click **OK**.

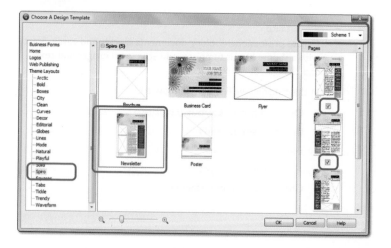

User Details

When you create a publication from a theme layout, you'll be prompted to update your **User Details**. These details are stored so that you only need to update them once. Let's do this now.

To update User Details

1 On the **Business** tab, complete the details required. (We've created a fictional company and address.)

2 Click **Update**.

The publication updates with the new details.

3 To change the details, click 🗐 Set User Details and make your changes in the dialog.

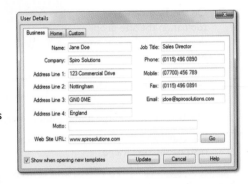

Page 1 opens in the workspace. You can see both pages displayed on the **Pages** tab.

• Double-click on page 2 to display it in the workspace.

At the bottom-left of page 2, you can see that the user details have been updated with the information that you've just entered. However, in our example the email address wraps onto the next line. Let's amend this.

To change font size

1 Click to the left of the word SPIRO and drag to highlight all of the text in the frame.

2 On the Text context toolbar, in the size drop-down list, set the font size to 8 pt.

Company Deta ▾ BacktalkSerif BTN ▾ | 8 pt ▾ | **B** /

The text now fits in the frame without wrapping.

We could give the text even more space by resizing the text frame.

To resize and centre a text frame

1 Click on the border of the text frame to select it. The selected border turns grey.

2 Click on the centre-left handle and drag it to the left to increase the width of the text frame.

3 Position the pointer just above and to the left of the coloured rectangle. Click and drag a marquee around both objects to select them.

4 On the **Align** tab, select Relative to: **Selection** and then, click
   Centre Vertically and
   Centre Horizontally.

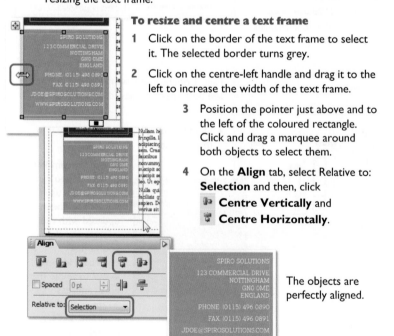

The objects are perfectly aligned.

Adding images

The themed layouts provide placeholder picture frames for you to add your own photos. We'll do this now.

To add images

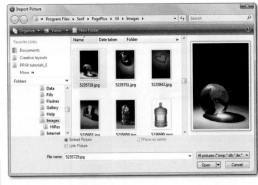

1 On the **Pages** tab, double-click on page 1 to display it in the workspace.

2 Position the pointer over the first empty frame and click to select it. The ![icon] **Replace Picture** button displays below the frame.

3 Click ![icon] **Replace Picture**.

4 The **Import Picture** dialog opens. Navigate to the picture that you want to use, click to select it, and then click **Open**.

The picture is placed in the frame and the Picture Frame toolbar displays beneath it. You can use this to adjust your picture inside its frame. We'll try this now.

To pan an image

1 Click the ![icon] **Pan** tool.

2 Click and drag the image with the ![icon] **Pan** cursor.

3 Release the mouse button when you are happy with the position of the image.

We can use the same toolbar to adjust the zoom of the image within the frame.

To zoom an image

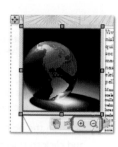

- Click the ⊕ **Zoom In** button to zoom in.
- Click the ⊖ **Zoom Out** button to zoom out.

Let's add an image to the other empty picture frames. This time we'll use the **Media Bar**.

To add images with the Media Bar

1 At the bottom of the workspace, click the ▬▬▲ handle to expand the **Media Bar**.

2 In the drop-down list, select an album. We chose PagePlus X4 Template Images 1.

3 Scroll to the image you want to add (or search for it in the search bar).

4 Drag the thumbnail onto the picture frame on the page.

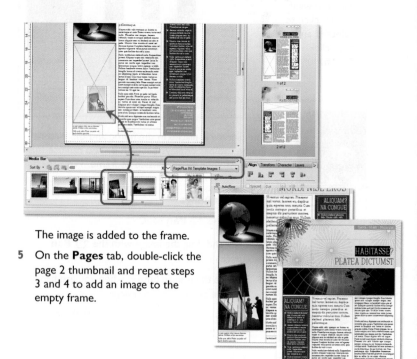

The image is added to the frame.

5 On the **Pages** tab, double-click the page 2 thumbnail and repeat steps 3 and 4 to add an image to the empty frame.

> For more information on using the **Media Bar**, see the **How To** tab or online Help. For more about images in general, take a look at the *Pictures* tutorial later in this section.

Let's now have a go at editing some text. On the **Pages** tab, double-click on Page 1.

To edit text

1 Click and drag to select the text 'SAPIEN VITAE?'.

2 Type 'SPIRO SOLUTIONS'.

The original text is replaced but the current formatting is retained.

3 Triple-click to select the second title line.

4 Type 'WINTER 2009'.

Once again, the original formatting is retained.

You may also want to change the appearance of your text. Let's demonstrate this now.

To format text

1 Select the text 'WINTER 2009.'

2 On the Text context toolbar, in the font drop-down list, select a different font. We chose **Egyptian710 BT**.

3 On the **Swatches** tab, ensure that ⚊ **Text** is selected and then, click the **Scheme Colour 2** swatch. The text is updated.

💡 You can use any colour swatch to colour your text. However, by using a scheme colour, the text will update to match the colour scheme applied.

To conclude this tutorial, let's change the colour scheme to one that better suits our seasonal publication.

To change the colour scheme

• On the **Schemes** tab, click to select **Scheme 2**.

All schemed objects within publication update with the new colours.

That concludes this tutorial. You should now be feeling familiar with the tools and techniques required to turn a theme layout into your own custom publication.

For more detailed information on working with text, pictures, and colour schemes, take a look at the other tutorials in this section.

Frame Text

This tutorial shows how to create and manipulate frame text.
We'll show you how to:

- Create, edit, and format text frames and text.

- Create placeholder text.

- Link text between frames.

- Use layout guides.

- Change scheme colours.

Frame Text

PagePlus provides two types of text—*frame text* and *artistic text*. Frame text is placed on the page inside a *text frame*, and is generally used for body copy and longer passages of text, or non-decorative text such as contact details, product information, etc.

Artistic text is most often used for titles and decorative text. For more on artistic text, see the *Artistic Text* tutorial.

Frame text has several special properties. It enables you to:

- Flow text between linked frames.
- Wrap text around pictures and shapes.
- Shape the frame to page objects.

In this tutorial, we'll show you how to create and manipulate frame text. We'll be working with one of the design templates included with PagePlus.

To open a themed layout

1 On the **File** menu, click **New from Startup Wizard**.

   In the Startup Wizard, click the **Use Design Template** option.

2 In the dialog:

   - In the **Theme Layouts** list on the left, select the **Spiro** category.

   - In the centre pane, select the **Newsletter** template.

   - In the **Pages** pane, select pages 2, 3 and 4, then clear the page 1 option.

   - Click **OK**.

3 In the **User Details** dialog click **Update**.

The template opens as a new, three page document in the workspace. Each page is displayed in the **Pages** tab (illustrated right).

The methods described in the following sections are applicable to both artistic and frame text, however, in this tutorial, we will concentrate on frame text.

To begin, we'll show you how to select, edit, and format text.

To select and edit text

1   Click on the title 'HABITASSE' at the top of the page.

The HintLine toolbar tells you that this is a *text frame*.

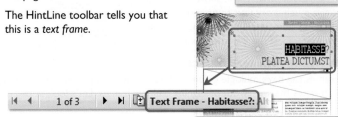

2   Click to place an insertion point before the 'H' and then drag to the right to select the entire top line of text.

3   Type 'SPIRO SOLUTIONS'.

4   Triple-click on the second line of text to select it.

5   Type 'WINTER 2009.'

Well done, the title is complete and you've now used two methods to select text! Let's move on to look at some of the ways we can edit a text frame.

Linked frames

In PagePlus, you can link multiple text frames. This allows the text to flow from one frame to another automatically. If a frame is linked, when selected, a  **Link** button displays at the bottom right of the frame. When you delete a linked frame, the story text is moved to the next linked frame.

1 Select the rightmost text frame on the page and press **Delete**.

2 Select the centre frame again.

The centre frame now shows two different buttons, ⊞ **AutoFlow** and ☐ **Overflow**. These show that there is too much story text to fit in the current frame. We'll tell you more about the function of the frame buttons later.

Working with text frames

Frames can have multiple columns. This can help simplify the layout design as it takes the worry out of aligning multiple frames. Let's look at this now.

To change the frame layout

1 With the frame selected, click and drag the centre right resize handle to the right-hand margin. The text expands to fill the frame.

2 On the Text context toolbar, set the column number to **2**.

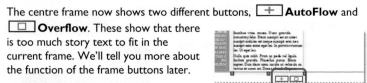

The text frame updates to contain 2 columns.

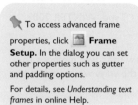

To access advanced frame properties, click 🖼 **Frame Setup.** In the dialog you can set other properties such as gutter and padding options.

For details, see *Understanding text frames* in online Help.

Next we'll add a familiar 'drop caps' format to the first paragraph.

To add drop caps formatting to text

1 Double-click to select the first word in the first paragraph of the text frame.

2 In the **Format** menu, click **Drop Cap...**

3 In the **Text Style** dialog:

   - Set the **Drop cap type:** to **Dropped**.

   - Click **OK** to accept the default settings.

   The drop cap style is applied to the first paragraph.

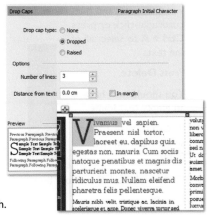

To select, copy and paste text

1 Triple-click on the longest paragraph in the text frame. The entire paragraph is selected.

2 On the Standard toolbar, click 🗐 **Copy** (or press **Ctrl + C**).

3 Click anywhere in the text frame to create an insertion point. (As we are working with placeholder text you don't have to be accurate.)

4 Click 🗐 **Paste** (or press **Ctrl + V**). The text is inserted.

   The frame button has changed to indicate that we now have more story text than the text frame can hold. Let's fix this by linking the frame.

5 On the **Pages** tab, double-click page 2 to display it in the workspace.

6 Click in the centre frame to create an insertion point and then either quadruple-click or press **Ctrl + A** to select all of the text.

7 Press **Delete**.

You should now have an empty text frame.

8 Return to page 1 and select the main text frame.

9 Click the [▢] **Overflow** button.

The [cursor icon] cursor appears.

10 Return to page 2 and click once in the empty frame.

The hidden overflow text from the previous frame on page 1 appears as the two frames are now linked.

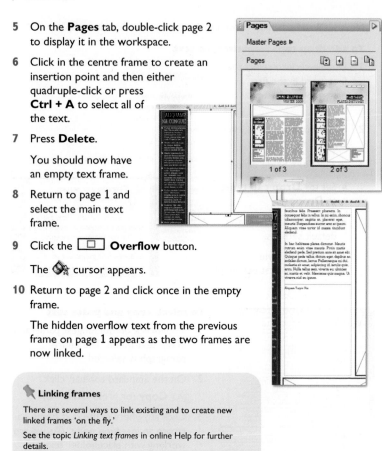

> **Linking frames**
>
> There are several ways to link existing and to create new linked frames 'on the fly.'
>
> See the topic *Linking text frames* in online Help for further details.

For our final example, we're going to get a little more creative. Click on page 3 in the **Pages** tab and let's begin!

Before we dive in and start changing the design elements, we'll introduce one of the most useful tools in desktop publishing, the **layout grid**.

A layout grid is a set of non-printing guides that can help you to consistently place and align images. Using the grid can really enhance your layouts. Here, we'll show you how to create a 5 x 5 grid, however, if you want to know more, see the tutorials, *Designing on a Grid* and *Creating Grid Layouts*.

To create a layout grid

1   On the Pages context toolbar, click
    ⊞ Layout Guides .

2   In the dialog:

    • Set the **Rows** to **5**.

    • Set the **Columns** to **5**.

    • Click **OK**.

    The grid appears on the page.

The first thing that you'll notice is that the current layout of the objects does not match the new grid layout. We'll use some of the techniques used earlier and some new techniques to change this.

To delete multiple unwanted frames

1   Click on the workspace just above the purple pull quote. Click and drag a section marquee around the pull quote objects and the centre text frame.

2   Press **Delete**.

You are left with the frame on the left of the page and the objects at the bottom.

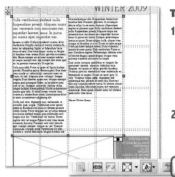

To change the frame layout

1 Click to select the left-most frame, drag the centre right resize handle to expand the frame over four layout columns.

 The text expands to fill the frame.

2 On the Text context toolbar, set the column number to **2**.

 The text frame updates to contain 2 columns.

The pull quotes in this theme layout have been created by placing text frames on top of filled QuickShapes. However, an alternative method is to create a colour-filled text frame.

To create a colour-filled text frame

1 On the Tools toolbar, click the
 Standard Text Frame.

2 On the page, align the mouse pointer with the edge of the rightmost layout column. Click and drag on the page to create a text frame that fits inside the layout column and is approximately 15.5 cm high.

3 Select the border of the frame and on the **Swatches** tab, click the **Fill** button and then click the **Scheme Colour 3** swatch.

 The fill is applied.

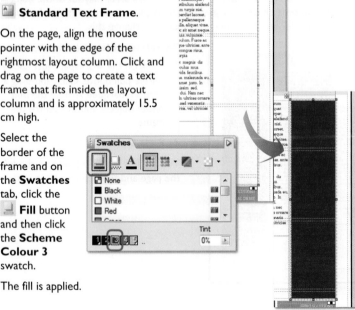

To create placeholder text

1 Click inside the text frame to create an insertion point, and then type the word 'TIPS'. Press **Enter** to drop to the next line.

2 On the **Insert** menu, click **Fill with Placeholder Text** (or press **F5**).

3 Triple-click to select the longest paragraph and press **Delete**.

4 Next, click to place an insertion point at the end of each placeholder sentence and press **Enter**.

This will become our placeholder bullet text. Don't worry if you can't see it very well at the moment, we'll fix this in the next step.

To format text using text styles

1 Press **Ctrl +A** to select all of the text in the frame.

2 On the Text context toolbar, in the styles drop-down list, select **Bullet List**.

The style is applied to the text.

3 Next, double-click the word 'TIPS'.

4 On the Text context toolbar, in the styles drop-down list, select **Bullet List Heading Left**.

The style is applied.

If you use styles to format text as we have done here, you have the advantage that if you want to change the style, all instances of that formatting also update.

Let's try this now.

To update a text style

1 With the word 'TIPS' still selected, on the **Swatches** tab, click the ⬛ **Fill** button and then click the **Scheme Colour 1** swatch.

A fill is placed behind the text.

2   Right-click the selected text and in the **Text Format** menu, click **Update Text Style**.

3   In the warning dialog, click **Yes** to confirm the update to the style in the entire document.

4   Finally, navigate to the other pages in the document. Notice that all of the bullet headings have been updated to match.

At the moment, the text extends right to the edges of the text frame. While this is what we want normally, it can look a little odd when the frame has a colour fill. We can fix this by **padding** the frame.

To add frame padding

1   Navigate to page 3 again and select the newly created text frame.

2   On the Text context toolbar, click **Frame Setup**.

3   In the dialog:

    • On column 1, set the **Top** and **Bottom** to **0.2 cm**.

    • Set the **Left Margin** to **0.2 cm**.

    • Set the **Right Margin** to **0.2 cm**.

    • Click **OK**.

The frame is updated.

To finish this tutorial, we'll illustrate why we used scheme colours to colour our text and text frames.

When you switch to a different scheme, any elements in the publication that have been assigned one of the scheme colour numbers are updated with the corresponding colour from the new scheme. This means that we can give our newsletter a completely new look without any hard work!

To change the colour scheme

- On the **Schemes** tab, click to select a different scheme. (We chose **Abstract**.)

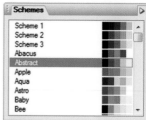

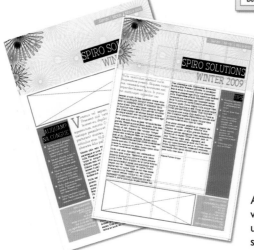

All of the schemed objects within the document update with the new scheme!

You now know how to edit and format text, create new frame text objects, and edit text frame properties.

The skills you have acquired should be sufficient for most of your projects, but you'll find more detailed information in online Help. If you haven't done so already, why not try the *Artistic Text* tutorial.

To find out more, and for help creating your own schemes, see the *Colour Schemes* tutorial.

Artistic Text

In this tutorial, we'll show you how to:

- Work with artistic text.
- Create, edit, and format text.
- Apply shadows, reflections, and other text effects.
- Create shaped text (or text-on-a-path).

Artistic Text

In this tutorial, we'll show you how to create and manipulate artistic text. Artistic text is standalone text that can be typed directly onto a page. Its special properties make it especially useful for titles, pull quotes, and other special-purpose text.

The special properties of artistic text allow you to:

- Stretch or squash the text to create a stylistic effect.
- Create shaped text by putting the text on a path.
- Apply instant 3D effects.

Over the next few pages, we'll create a poster using artistic text objects. Along the way, you'll learn how to apply some of the stunning visual effects available in PagePlus.

There are many professionally designed templates, including the one used in this tutorial, available for PagePlus. Please contact Serif for details.

To open a design template

1 On the **File** menu, click **New from Startup Wizard**.

2 In the Startup Wizard, click the **Use Design Template** option.

3 In the dialog, select a category from the left pane to display the available publications.

4 In the centre pane, click the publication thumbnail then click **OK**.

The template opens as a new publication in the workspace.

To open a themed layout:

1 On the Standard toolbar, click 📂 **Open** or from the Startup Wizard, select **Open Saved Publication**.

2 Browse to the ...**Workspace\\Text** folder and open the **artistic.ppp** file. In a standard installation, you'll find this folder in the following location:

C:\\Program Files\\Serif\\PagePlus\\X4\\Tutorials

3 The document opens in the workspace.

Although we are working with artistic text in this tutorial, many of the methods described below are applicable to both artistic and frame text.

As we are concentrating on purely artistic text objects, let's delete the frame text that is currently on the poster.

To select and delete text frames

1 Using the 🔨 **Pointer Tool**, click to select the 'EXTREME GEAR' text object located at the top of the poster.

2 In the lower-left corner of the workspace, the HintLine toolbar tells us that this is *frame text*.

3 Press and hold the **Shift** key and click on each text frame to select them all at the same time.

4 Press the **Delete** key.

Now let's create a new artistic text object...

To create artistic text

1 On the Tools toolbar, on the
   A ▾ Text flyout, click the A **Artistic Text Tool**.

2 Click anywhere on your page to set a text insertion point.

3 On the Text context toolbar, in the Text Styles drop-down list, select **TITLE COL**.

4 Type 'EXTREME GEAR'.

Now that our basic title is placed, let's make it a little more interesting.

To accurately resize and rotate artistic text

1 With the text object still selected, on the **Transform** tab, ensure that the ⊹ **Lock Aspect Ratio** is off. (If not, click the button once.)

2 Change the Width to **28.0 cm** and then change the Height to **13.0 cm**.

3 Finally, rotate the object by **5°**.

4 Click and drag the ✥ **Move** button located just above the upper-left corner of the object (or click and drag on the object's border) to drag the object into position as illustrated.

The title already has a lot more impact, but we can make it even more powerful by adding a gradient fill.

To apply a gradient fill

1   With the text still selected, go to the **Swatches** tab.

2   Expand the **Gradient Fills** flyout and select **Linear**.

3   Click the **Linear Fill 14** swatch to apply it to the text.

The gradient colour spread works well, but we can make it fit the overall colour scheme better by changing it to use scheme colours.

To edit a gradient fill

1   Select the text object and then on the Tools toolbar, click the **Fill Tool**.

The object's fill path is displayed.

2   On the Fill context toolbar:

•   In the **Fill Start** drop-down list, select swatch 5 on the Scheme 5 row.

•   In the **Fill End** drop-down list, select swatch 5 on the Scheme 4 row.

3   (Optional) You can also adjust the fill path by clicking and dragging the fill path nodes.

The title is almost complete; however, let's make it look really special by adding a reflection effect.

To apply a reflection effect

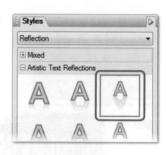

1 With the text object selected, go to the **Styles** tab and in the categories drop-down list, select **Reflection**.

2 In the **Artistic Text Reflections** sub-category, click the **Text Reflection 03 : FilterEffects** preset.

The reflection is applied.

To edit a reflection effect

1 With the text object selected, on the Attributes toolbar, click the *fx* **Filter Effects** button.

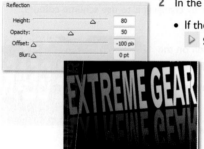

2 In the dialog:

- If the preview is not displayed, click ▷ **Show/Hide Preview**.

  - Drag the **Offset** slider to the left until the reflection sits just below the text.

  - Click **OK**.

  The reflection is updated.

The next thing we need to add is our tag-line. Once again, we shall use an artistic text object, but this time, we'll apply an **Instant 3D** style.

To create 3D text

1 On the Tools toolbar, on the A ▾ Text flyout, click the A **Artistic Text Tool**.

2 Click and drag anywhere on your page to create a text insertion point approximately 55 pt.

3 On the **Swatches** tab, click the ⚊ **Text** button and then click the **Scheme Colour 3** swatch.

4 Type 'gear with attitude'.

5 With the text object still selected, go to the **Styles** tab, and in the categories drop-down list, click **3D**.

6 In the **Mixed** sub-category, click the **3D 06 : Warp** preset.

The effect is applied.

7 Click and drag the ✛ **Move** button to drag the object into position so that it is just overlapping the title text as illustrated.

🔖 To edit the text in an instant 3D object, select the object and click ▭. The text displays with a coloured outline. To select all of the text, press **Ctrl + A**; to select a word or range of text, click and drag. You can now format the text style, font, size, colour etc. in the usual way.

For more information about Instant 3D, see the topic *Adding dimensionality (Instant 3D)* in online Help.

For the final step, we are going to add the company website URL to the poster. For that extra special touch, we'll create it on a curved path.

To place text on a path

1   On the Tools toolbar, on the A ▾ Text flyout, click the A **Artistic Text Tool**.

2   Click anywhere on your page to create a text insertion point and on the Text context toolbar, set the font size to **48 pt**.

3   Go to the **Swatches** tab, click the $\underline{\mathrm{A}}$ **Text** button and then click the **Scheme Colour 4** swatch. Set the **Tint** to **-50%**.

4   On the **Insert** menu, select **Information > User Details...**

5   In the dialog, select **Work Web** and click **OK**.

The company URL stored in the **User Details** is inserted on the page.

User details provide a quick and easy way to update any personal or work details within a document. To set or update your details, click 🔲🔲 Set User Details on the Pages context toolbar. For more information, see the topic *Inserting user details* in online Help.

6 On the Text context toolbar, in the ✕ ▾ **Path Text** drop-down list, select **Path - Wave**.

7 To stretch the path, drag the Start and End nodes (red highlight).

8 To adjust the slope of the path, click on a Start or End node and then drag its curve handle (yellow highlight).

9 (Optional) Resize the text object by clicking and dragging the top and side edge resize handles.

10 Finally, click and drag the ✛ **Move** button to move the object into position just below and to the left of the two images.

The poster is complete! However, we'll take this opportunity to illustrate why we used scheme colours to colour our text...

To change the colour scheme

- On the **Schemes** tab, click to select a different scheme.

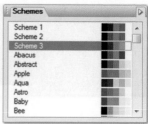

All of the schemed objects update!

This makes it easy to change the overall look and feel of your publication without any extra work. To find out more, and for help creating your own schemes, see the *Colour Schemes* tutorial.

We hope that you've enjoyed this tutorial. You should now be quite adept at using artistic text. If you haven't done so already, why not try the *Frame Text* tutorial? Have fun!

Pictures

The right pictures can make your publication stand out from the crowd.

In this tutorial, we'll show you how to:

- Add and replace pictures.
- Use the **Media Bar**.
- Pan, zoom, and crop pictures.
- Apply image adjustments.
- Apply wrap to an image.
- Insert an inline image.

Pictures

PagePlus offers a variety of tools and techniques for working with the pictures within your publication. In this tutorial, we'll start with a themed layout, then we'll show you how to add your own pictures, crop them, apply some basic image adjustments, and wrap text around the picture.

We'll be using the sample images installed with PagePlus. In a standard installation, you'll find this folder in the following location:

C:\Program Files\Serif\PagePlus\X4\Images

You can use your own images if you prefer.

To open a themed layout

1   On the **File** menu, click **New from Startup Wizard**.

2   Click the **Use Design Template** option.

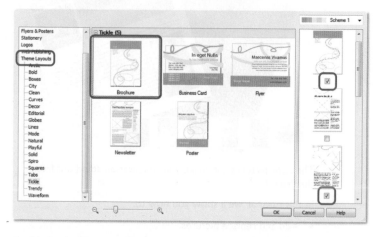

3   In the dialog, in the left pane, click to expand **Themed Layouts** then click the **Tickle** category.

4   In the centre pane, click the **Brochure** thumbnail.

5   In the right **Pages** pane, select pages **1** and **3**.

6   Click **OK**.

The layout opens in the workspace.

Before we do anything else, we'll customize the title.

1 Click and drag on the word 'Integer' to select it.

2 Type 'Getting away from it all...'

Our title is complete! Let's move on and start adding some pictures.

On the **Pages** tab, double-click the page 2 thumbnail to display the page in the workspace.

Adding pictures

This themed layout page provides three placeholder picture frames for you to add your own photos.

You can add pictures individually by clicking directly on a placeholder, or you can add multiple pictures to the **Media Bar** and then drag them onto the frames as you need them. We'll demonstrate both methods.

To add a single picture to a frame

1 Click to select the large picture frame, then click the 🖼 **Replace Picture** button in the lower-right corner of the frame.

2 In the **Import Picture** dialog, browse to your **Images** folder.

3 Select the **34590800.jpg** file and click **Open**.

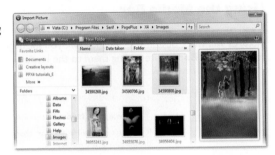

The picture is added to the frame and scaled to fit.

When the picture is selected, note that the **Picture Frame** toolbar displays in the lower-right corner. You can use these tools to adjust your picture inside the frame.

To adjust a picture inside a frame

- To reposition the picture inside the frame, click ⬛ **Pan**, and then click and drag on the picture with the ⬛ **Pan** cursor.

- To rotate the picture counter-clockwise, in 90° increments, click ⬛ **Rotate**.

- To zoom in or out of the picture, click ⊕ **Zoom In** or ⊖ **Zoom Out**, and then click on the picture.

- To replace the picture, click ⬛ **Replace Picture**, browse to and select a new picture and click **Open**.

Using the Media Bar

If you're working with lots of pictures, or are not sure which of your pictures will work best in your publication, you might prefer to add them to the **Media Bar** before adding them to the layout.

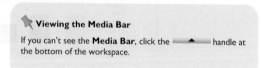

Viewing the Media Bar

If you can't see the **Media Bar**, click the ▬▬▲▬▬ handle at the bottom of the workspace.

 **Using the Media Bar**

By default, pictures are added to a temporary album, but you can also create more permanent albums from which you can retrieve stored images at any time.

For details, see the **How To** tab or the online Help.

To add images to the Media Bar

1 By default, the **Media Bar**, displays a **Temporary Album**. If not, select this in the rightmost drop-down list.

2 Click in the blank area of the tab.

- or -

Click 🖻 **Add Image**.

In the **Import Picture** dialog, navigate to your **Images** folder.

3 Press and hold down the **Ctrl** key and select the following files:

34590800.jpg, 39192192.jpg, 4579195.jpg, 5117743.jpg, 5804618.jpg and 6301388.jpg

4 Click **Open**.

The photos are displayed as thumbnails on the **Media Bar**.

5 Drag the photo of the wooded lake (39192192.jpg) onto the upper-right picture frame.

6 Drag the photo of the golfer (6301388.jpg) from the **Media Bar** onto the lower-left frame.

Once you've added pictures to frames, it's easy to replace them.

Let's change the top-right photo...

To replace a picture

- Drag the photo of the climber
  (4579195.jpg) from the **Media Bar**
  onto the upper-right frame.

  - or -

  Click the  **Replace Picture**
  button and browse to the new image.

The page is looking pretty good. Let's now have a
look at page 1. Along the way, we'll show you some
more image techniques. First of all, on the **Pages** tab,
double-click the page 1 thumbnail.

We're going to add a large image to this page, but first of all we need to
delete the elements that will obstruct our image.

To delete unwanted objects

1 (Optional) On the **View** toolbar,
  click 🖹 **Full Page**.

2 Position the pointer on the
  workspace in line with the 'Getting
  away from it all' text box.

3 Click and drag a selection marquee
  over all of the elements on the white
  section of the page.

4 Press the **Delete** key.

Now that we've created the
space, let's add an image.

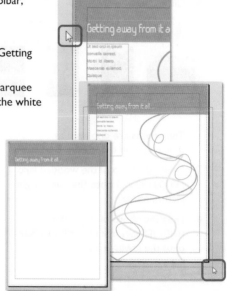

To insert a picture frame

1 On the Tools toolbar, on the
   ▣ ▾ Picture flyout, click the
   ⊠ **Rectangular Picture Frame**.

2 Position the cursor at the left edge of
   the page, just below the green banner.
   Click and drag to create a frame that
   fills the 'white' area of the page.

3 Drag the photo of the mountain and
   rainbow (5117743.jpg) from the
   Media Bar onto the picture frame.

4 Click the ⊕ **Zoom In**
   button a couple of time to
   zoom into the image, then
   click the 🖑 **Pan** button
   to position the image so
   that the rainbow starts in
   the corner.

Applying image adjustments

When you select a picture, the Picture context toolbar displays at the top
of the workspace, automatically.

This toolbar provides quick and easy access to key picture-related
controls—replace, resize, recolour, and so on—and also lets you apply
useful image adjustments, such as red eye removal and brightness and
contrast adjustments, with a single click.

We can improve our cover photo by applying a contrast adjustment.

To apply an image adjustment

- With the picture frame selected, on the Picture context toolbar, click ☞ **Increase Contrast**. Repeat as required.

- (Optional) Experiment with the other adjustments provided on the Picture context toolbar to see how they effect the photos on your poster.

📌 **Advanced image adjustments**

PagePlus includes a powerful mix of advanced image correction and adjustment tools— including levels, colour balance, channel mixer, HSL, and Unsharp Mask—and a selection of creative effects such as Diffuse Glow and Gaussian Blur. All of these are applied from the **PhotoLab** dialog, which you can open by clicking ⊙ PhotoLab on the Picture context toolbar.

For more information, see online Help.

Creating anchored objects

If you are working with text and images in a publication, you can obtain fine control over object positioning using object anchoring. We'll introduce this by adding a small inline image to the cover title.

To add an inline image

1 Click on the **Gallery** tab and select the **Silhouettes** category.

2 In the **Birds** sub-category, drag **Bird3** onto the page.

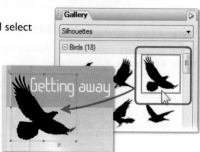

3 Resize the silhouette so that it fits the size of the text. If you haven't done so already, drag it into position next to the title.

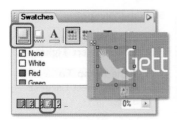

4 Click on the **Swatches** tab, and change the ▭ **Fill** colour to **Scheme Colour 4**.

5 On the **Arrange** menu, click **Anchor Object...**

6 In the **Anchored Objects Properties** dialog:

- Select **Position inline as character**.

- In the **Align with text** drop-down list, select **Middle**.

- Click **OK**.

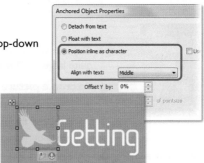

The image is anchored to the text as an inline character.

That completes the font cover.

Applying wrap settings

To finish the tutorial we'll look at wrapping text around an image. Let's add another image to page 2.

To apply wrap settings

1 On the **Pages** tab, double-click the page 2 thumbnail.

2 Drag the tennis image (5804618.jpg) from the **Media Bar** onto the page.

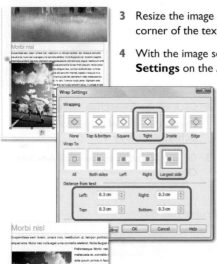

3   Resize the image so that it fits in the bottom-left corner of the text frame.

4   With the image selected, click ▣ **Wrap Settings** on the **Arrange** toolbar.

5   In the **Wrapping** dialog:

- In the **Wrapping** section, select **Tight**.

- In the **Wrap To** section, select **Largest Side**.

- In the **Distance from text** section, enter **0.3 cm** in all four of the value boxes.

- Click **OK**.

The text wraps around the image. As this image is quite large, we'll finish by applying a crop.

To crop a picture

1   Select the photo of the tennis player, then on the Crop flyout, click the ⊡ **Square Crop Tool**.

2   Click and drag the right edge handle inwards, as illustrated, and the top handle downwards, so that there are three lines of text above the image.

3   (Optional) To reposition a cropped image inside its frame, click and drag on the image (the cursor temporarily changes to ✋ **Pan**).

That's it! We've reached the end of this tutorial on pictures. We hope that you have enjoyed working through these simple exercises.

You should be much more familiar with the techniques we've explored and able to confidently add pictures to your own publications.

Styles and Objects

Turn a simple holiday snap into a work of art with these simple steps.

In this tutorial, we will:

- Add a pre-built picture frame to an image.
- Add a drop shadow effect.
- Apply pre-defined styles to objects and text.

Styles and Objects

PagePlus offers a variety of pre-built objects and styles to help you to easily enhance your text and images. Over the next few pages, we'll give you a brief introduction to this by embellishing a holiday photo. Let's get started!

New publication

1   From the Startup Wizard, click **Start New Publication**.

2   In the leftmost pane, select **Landscape** from the **Regular/Normal** category.

3   In the large pane, click to select the **A4** or **Letter** thumbnail.

4   Click **OK**.

A new blank document opens in the workspace.

To add a Gallery picture frame to an image

1   On the Tools toolbar, click 🖼 **Import Picture**.

2   In the **Import Picture** dialog, browse to your chosen image, click to select it and then click **Open**.

3   Position the mouse pointer inside the page margin guide, then, click and drag to place your image on the page.

We used image **5117743.jpg**, a stock image provided with PagePlus installation. In a default installation, you'll find this and many other images in the following location:

C:\Program Files\Serif\PagePlus\X4\Images

4   On the **Align** tab:

*   In the **Relative to:** drop-down list, select **Page**.

*   Click **Centre Horizontally**.

*   Click **Centre Vertically**.

5   On the **Gallery** tab, in the **Picture Frames** category, in the **Fun** sub-category, click and drag the **Bamboo** frame thumbnail onto the image.

The frame is added.

6   To change the frame, simply drag a different thumbnail onto the image.

Here, we replaced the **Bamboo** frame with the **Pipes** frame from the **Metallic** sub-category.

To add a drop shadow

1 With your image selected, click on the **Styles** tab.

2 In the category drop-down list, select **Shadows**.

3 In the **Drop Shadow** sub-category, click on a style thumbnail to apply it.

Let's now add some artistic text to our holiday photo. We'll then apply one of the styles in the **Styles** tab.

To apply style formatting to text

1 On the Tools toolbar, click the A **Artistic Text Tool**.

2 Click on the lower-left corner of the image to create an insertion point.

3 On the Text context toolbar, set the font to **Arial Black** and the size to **36 pt**.

4 Type 'CANADA 09'.

5 Click the text frame border to select it.

6 On the **Styles** tab, select the **Presets - Materials** category from the drop-down list.

7 In the **Glass** sub-category, click the **Glass 01** thumbnail.

The effect is applied to the text.

To apply style formatting to a Gallery object

1   Click on the **Gallery** tab and select the **Silhouettes** category.

2   Scroll to the **Plants & Floral** sub-category and then drag the maple leaf silhouette on to the page.

3   Drag on the upper corner handle to resize the object so that it fits in with the text. Reposition as necessary.

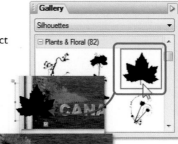

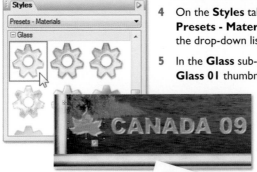

4   On the **Styles** tab, select the **Presets - Materials** category from the drop-down list.

5   In the **Glass** sub-category, click the **Glass 01** thumbnail.

The object updates to match the style of the text.

That's it! Using the **Gallery** and **Styles** tabs we've created a stunning holiday snapshot. Why not apply some of these techniques to your own images? Have fun!

Master Pages

Some elements of your design will appear on every page of your publication. For a professional look, these elements should be placed consistently from page to page. By using master pages, you can save yourself time and effort as you only need to place the elements once. If you need a different design for certain pages, simply create additional master pages!

In this tutorial, we'll show you how to enhance the design of a tri-fold layout by using master pages. You'll learn how to:

- Add a company logo to a master page.
- Work with images and backgrounds.
- Create a watermark.
- Add a page number.
- Work with multiple master pages.

Master Pages

When you add text frames, pictures, or other elements to the master page, they appear in the same position on all document pages based on that master page. Any content that is placed on normal pages appears on top of the master page elements. This makes it easy to create a consistent design throughout your publication.

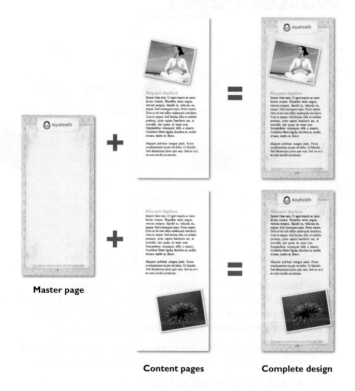

Master page

Content pages

Complete design

Every new document that you open in PagePlus includes one default master page, **Master A**. However, you can also create multiple master pages, each having different page elements, which you can then assign to the various pages of your publication. This means that you can have different, but consistent, page layouts within the same publication.

Master pages simplify document maintenance as objects placed on a master page only need updating once. (If you didn't use a master page, you'd have to update the object on each individual page of the document.)

To demonstrate master pages, we've created a simple tri-fold flyer, **flyer.ppp**, which you can find in your **Workspace\Flyer** folder. We'll enhance the layout by applying a background design with a master page.

To open the workspace document

1 Click **File**, then **Open**—or from the Startup Wizard, select **Open Saved Publication**.

2 Browse to the ...**Workspace\Flyer** folder and open the **flyer.ppp** file. In a standard installation, you'll find this file in the following location:

C:\Program Files\Serif\PagePlus\X4\Tutorials

> **Tri-fold flyer**
>
> We've already created placeholder content within this document. However, to create a tri-fold flyer from scratch:
>
> 1 From the **Startup Wizard**, click **Start New Publication**.
>
> 2 Click the **Folded** category.
>
> 3 Click **Side Z-fold Menu**.
>
> 4 Click **OK**.

Before we start, take a moment to familiarize yourself with the document layout by double-clicking the pages in the **Pages** tab.

Notice that the document currently has a single, blank master page. Let's edit this now.

To create a master page background

1 On the **Pages** tab, expand the **Master Pages** category and double-click the 'Master A' page thumbnail to display the page in the workspace.

2 On the Tools toolbar, in the ⬚ ▾ Picture flyout, click the ⊠ **Rectangular Picture Frame**.

3 Click and drag from the top left corner of the page to the bottom right to place the frame so that it covers the entire page.

4 At the bottom of the frame, click the 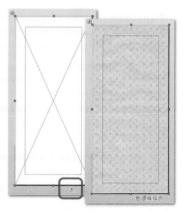 button and in the dialog, browse to the **Flyer** folder. Click the **Tiled Leaf Background.jpg** and click **Open**.

The background is placed inside the frame.

5 On the Tools toolbar, click the ⊠ **Rectangular Picture Frame**.

6 Click and drag on the page to place another frame, approximately 9 cm x 20 cm.

7 With the frame selected, on the **Align** tab, click ⊞ **Centre Horizontally**; in the **Relative to:** drop-down list, ensure that **Page** is selected.

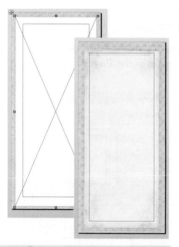

8 Click the button and in the dialog, open **panel_half.png**.

By default, the image is cropped to best fit. For this type of image, we can change the settings so that the entire image is sized to fit the frame.

9 On the Picture context toolbar:

- Click ⊞ Frame Properties .

- In the dialog, click **Stretch to Fit** and click **OK**.

10 Finally, we'll place a smaller panel to hold our logo. Click the ⊠ **Rectangular Picture Frame** and drag on the page to place a small, 6 cm x 2 cm frame at the top of the page.

11 Click the button and in the dialog, open **panel_quarter.png** and adjust the alignment and frame properties as before.

Now to add our logo...

To add a logo from the Gallery

1   On the **Gallery** tab, select the **Logos** category from the drop-down menu.

2   Scroll down to **logo 80**, then click and drag it from the tab onto the page.

    The **Insert Logo** dialog opens.

3   In the dialog:

    • Clear the **Apply colour set** option.

    • In the **Designs** pane, click the third design down.

    • In the **Name** text box, type 'Aquahealth'.

    • Clear the text from the **Motto** text box

    • Click **OK**.

    The logo is placed on the page.

4   Move the logo into position over the small panel and resize as necessary.

    The logo is almost complete, but let's change the text to match the logo colour. We can do this easily in **LogoStudio**.

To edit a logo in LogoStudio

1   With the logo selected, click the 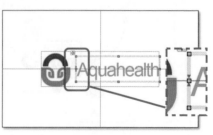 **Edit in LogoStudio** button. The logo opens for editing in **LogoStudio**.

2   Click to select the text object and then, with the **Move** button, drag it down into a central position. The object should snap to the centre guideline.

3   On the Text context toolbar, set the font to **Trebuchet MS** and set the size to **18 pt**.

4   On the Attributes toolbar, click the **Fill Tool**.

5   On the Fill context toolbar:

   • Set the fill type to **Linear**.

   • In the **Fill Start** drop-down list, select swatch 5 on the Scheme 2 row.

   • In the **Fill End** drop-down list, select swatch 5 on the Scheme 3 row.

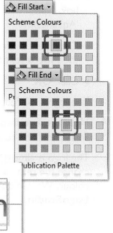

6   Finally, drag the nodes into the position illustrated below so that the gradient goes from top to bottom.

7   Click **Close LogoStudio** to return to the main PagePlus workspace.

Our master page is almost complete. Let's finish by adding contact details and a page number.

To add contact details

1   On the Tools toolbar, click the 📄▾ **Standard Text Frame**.

2   Click and drag on the page to place a frame approximately 8.5 cm wide and 0.5 cm high.

3   Go to the **Text Styles** tab (at the left of the workspace) and click the **Footer** paragraph style.

    (If you can't see the **Footer** style, select the **Show All** option.)

4   In the text frame, type 'To make an appointment call', and then click **Insert > Information > User Details...**

5   In the dialog, select **Work Phone** from the list and click **OK**. The phone number is added to the text frame.

6   Finally, drag the text frame into position at the bottom of the page.

To add a page number

1   On the Tools toolbar, click the 📄▾ **Standard Text Frame**.

2   Click and drag on the page to place a frame approximately 1.5 cm wide and 0.7 cm high.

3   On the **Text Styles** tab, click the **Emphasis** character style.

4   On the **Insert** menu, click **Page Number**.

5   On the Text context toolbar, click ≡ **Align Centre**.

6   Finally, drag the frame into position at the bottom of the document, below the previous frame.

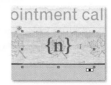

To return to normal view

1 Double-click a normal page thumbnail on the **Pages** tab.

2 Click through pages on the **Pages** tab, or click the arrows on the Hintline toolbar, to view the pages.

Front page

Inner pages

The design suits the inner pages well, but it looks a little boring for the cover of the folded flyer. What we need is a different design for the front and back pages. We can easily do this by creating a second master page, and we can save time and effort by reusing some of the work that we've already done!

💡 You can also quickly access your master pages from the Hintline toolbar.

- Click the **Current Page** button to display the currently assigned master page.

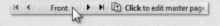

- Click the **Previous** and **Next** buttons to cycle through pages.
- Click the **Current Page** button again to return to normal view.

To create a second master page

1 On the **Pages** tab, double-click the 'Master A' page thumbnail to display the page in the workspace.

2 Click 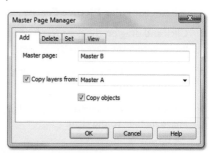 **Page Manager** and in the dialog:

   - Select the **Add** tab.

   - Select the **Copy layers from** option. The **Copy objects** option is selected by default.

   - Click **OK**.

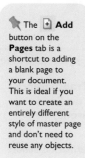 **The ⊞ Add** button on the **Pages** tab is a shortcut to adding a blank page to your document. This is ideal if you want to create an entirely different style of master page and don't need to reuse any objects.

The duplicate master page, **Master B**, is displayed in the workspace and as a thumbnail in the **Pages** tab.

Now we have our starting point, let's make some changes.

First let's delete the objects we don't need.

To delete multiple unwanted objects

1 On the Tools toolbar, click the ⬆ **Pointer Tool**.

2 Starting with the pointer on the workspace, drag a selection marquee around the 'contact' and 'page number' text frames at the bottom of the page. Both objects are selected.

3 Press the **Delete** key.

To add a watermark

1   On the Tools toolbar, in the  ▾ Picture flyout, click the ⊠ **Rectangular Picture Frame**.

2   Click and drag on the page to place a frame within the page margin guides.

3   Click the 🖾 button and in the dialog, open **yoga.png**.

4   Click the 👆 **Pan** button and pan the image further to the right.

5   On the **Transparency** tab, click the **Solid Transparency 70%** swatch.

The watermark is almost complete, but for a really professional look, we'll add a tint to match the colour scheme.

6   On the **Swatches** tab, click the ▭ **Fill** button and then click **Scheme Colour 4**.

7   To darken the colour, reduce the **Tint** value to **-50%**.

To complete the design, let's move the logo to the bottom of the page.

To adjust the logo

1   On the Tools toolbar, click the **Pointer Tool**.

2   Starting with the pointer on the workspace, drag a selection marquee around the panel and logo objects.

3   Click the **Group** button.

4   On the Arrange toolbar, click **Bring to Front**. The grouped logo object is brought in front of the image.

5   On the **Transform** tab, change the width to 9.5 cm. The height updates automatically as the aspect ratio is locked.

6   Finally, position the object so that the bottom edge is in line with the lower margin as illustrated.

Any grouped object that contains a LogoStudio logo will always have a locked aspect ratio.

Now we've completed our second master page design, we need to assign it to the front and back pages of our flyer.

To assign a master page

1 On the **Pages** tab, double-click on the 'Front' page thumbnail to return to normal view.

2 Click the ⬚ **Page Manager** button.

3 In the **Page Manager** dialog:

- Click the **Set** tab.

- In the **Publication page(s)** drop-down list, select 'Front.'

- In the **Uses master page** list, select 'Master B.'

- Click **OK**.

4 Repeat step 2 and 3 to assign 'Master B' to the 'Back' page.

To check master page assignment

- On the **Pages** tab, click ⬚ **Show Page Names**.

  The assigned master pages are displayed on each page thumbnail.

- Click the button again to return to the normal thumbnail view.

That's it! You have successfully created and assigned multiple master pages to a publication. Why not explore this technique in your own documents? Have fun!

⭐ For a detailed look at master pages, see the topics *Understanding master pages*, and the sub-topic *Working with layers: Layers and master pages* in online Help.

Colour Schemes

When designing your publications, one of the most important factors to consider is colour.

But how do you select a colour palette that's right for your publication? In this tutorial, we'll introduce you to the predesigned PagePlus colour schemes, which you can apply to any design element. If you take a look at our design templates, you'll notice that these are also designed to use colour schemes so that you can change the look and feel quickly and easily.

In this tutorial, you'll learn how to:

- Apply a preset colour scheme from the **Scheme Manager**.
- Modify an existing colour scheme.
- Create your own colour scheme from scratch.

Colour Schemes

In the first section of this tutorial, we'll apply scheme colours to individual elements on a page. We'll then show you how you can edit and modify scheme colours. Finally, we'll create a custom colour scheme from scratch. Let's get started...

Applying scheme colours to objects

You can apply a colour scheme at any point during the design process. Each publication can have just one colour scheme at a time and can easily switch from one to another.

To apply a colour scheme

1   Click **File**, then **Open**—or from the Startup Wizard, select **Open Saved Publication**.

    Browse to the ...**\Workspace\Colour Schemes** folder and open the **Health.ppp** file. In a standard installation, you'll find this file in the following location:

    C:\Program Files\Serif\PagePlus\X4\Tutorials

2   Click the **Schemes** tab.

    You'll see an assortment of named schemes, each consisting of five basic colours.

    The colour scheme that is currently applied throughout this publication is highlighted.

3   Right-click on the **Schemes** tab and select **Scheme Manager** (or click **Tools**, then **Scheme Manager**).

    In the **Scheme Manager** dialog, click the **Schemes** tab.

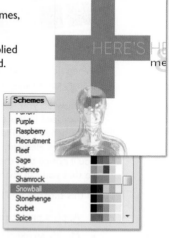

4   Click a few different colour schemes.

    As you select each new scheme, watch the **Preview** pane—you'll see various elements on the page change colour.

    So what exactly is happening here?

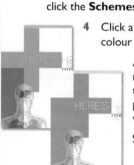

The scheme colours work much like a paint-by-numbers system, where various regions and elements of a page layout are coded with numbers. In each scheme, a specific colour is assigned to each number.

> When you save a publication, its current colour scheme is saved along with the PagePlus file.

When you switch to a different scheme, any elements in the publication that have been assigned one of the scheme colour numbers are updated with the corresponding colour from the new scheme.

Let's see this in action...

5   On the Tools toolbar, on the **QuickShape** flyout, click the **Quick Rectangle** and draw a large shape on the page.

6   Click to display the **Swatches** tab.

At the bottom of the tab, below the colour swatches, you'll see that the five main colours of the current colour scheme appear as numbered swatches.

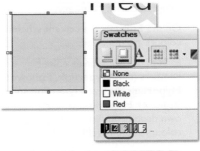

7   Select your shape. On the **Swatches** tab:

   • Click the **Fill** button and then click the scheme colour you want to apply to the shape's fill.

   • Click the **Line** button and apply a different scheme colour to the shape's outline.

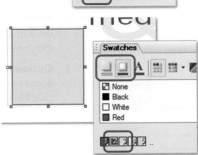

8 On the **Schemes** tab, click to apply a different colour scheme to the publication.

> If you copy an object that uses scheme colours to another PagePlus document, the object will take on the colour scheme used in the new document.

PagePlus applies the new scheme colours to the shape.

On the **Swatches** tab, notice that the colour scheme swatches have been replaced with the new scheme colours.

As you can see, when you create new elements in a PagePlus document, or create a new publication from scratch, you can extend a colour scheme to your layout elements using the process just described.

You'll need to spend some time working out which colour combinations look best, but the mechanics of the process are simple.

Modifying colour schemes

If you've tried various colour schemes but haven't found one that's quite right for your document, you can modify any of the colours in an existing scheme to create a new one.

To modify a colour scheme

1 Right-click on the **Schemes** tab and select **Scheme Manager**.

On the **Edit** tab, the current scheme colours are displayed.

Each of the five scheme colour numbers (plus **Hyperlink**, **Followed Hyperlink**, **Active Hyperlink** and **Rollover Hyperlink** colours) has its own drop-down list, showing available colours in the PagePlus palette.

2 To set or change a scheme colour, simply click the button to expand the drop-down list, and then select a new colour.

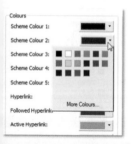

3 **Optional step:** If the drop-down palette doesn't contain the colour you want to use, click **More Colours** to display the **Colour Selector**.

💡 You can extend the **Colour Selector** dialog's publication palette using the **Palette Manager**, which lets you modify the current palette and also load and save named palettes.

For more information, see *Managing publication palettes* in online Help.

In the **Colour Selector** dialog, various controls allow you to choose a colour to apply or mix your own custom colours.

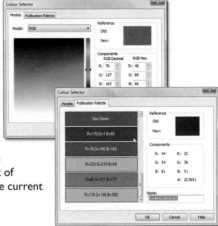

- The **Models** tab displays the colour space of the currently selected colour model.

- The **Publication Palette** tab lets you modify the set of colours associated with the current publication.

4   When you have modified your scheme on the **Edit** tab, save it by clicking **Save Scheme**.

🔑 The **Save Scheme** and **OK** buttons yield different results. Each PagePlus document stores a locally defined scheme, which may or may not correspond to a named scheme.

- Modifying a scheme in the **Scheme Manager** and then clicking **Save Scheme** updates the named scheme, but does not apply it to the publication.

- To ensure the publication uses the latest copy of the named scheme, click **OK** in the **Scheme Manager** or reapply the named scheme using the **Scheme Manager** or **Schemes** tab.

When modifying a scheme repeatedly, make sure your document is using the latest version.

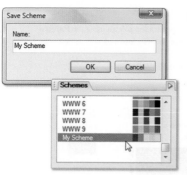

5 In the **Save Scheme** dialog:

- If you are modifying an existing scheme, leave the name unchanged and then click **OK**.

- If you are creating a new scheme, type in a new name and then click **OK**.

6 If you have saved your changes with a new name, click the **Schemes** tab and then scroll the list to locate the new colour scheme.

Creating custom colour schemes from scratch

There may be times when you want to create a new colour scheme from scratch, perhaps using colours from your company logo or an image that features in your PagePlus document or on your website.

To complete the following section, you can use our sample photograph or any image of your choice.

You'll find the sample photograph, **Cocktail.jpg**, in the **...\Workspace\Colour Schemes** folder of your PagePlus installation directory. In a standard installation, this folder is copied to the following location:

C:\Program Files\Serif\PagePlus\X4\Tutorials

To create a custom colour scheme from an image

1 On the Tools toolbar, click 🖼 **Import Picture** and browse to locate the image you want to use.

2 Click **Open** and position the image on your page.

3 Select the image and then on the Picture context toolbar, click ⊙ PhotoLab.

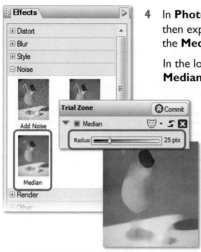

4   In **PhotoLab**, click the **Effects** tab and then expand the **Noise** category. Click the **Median** thumbnail.

In the lower right **Trial Zone**, the **Median** control displays,

5   Drag the **Radius** slider, to the right so that colours making up the image blend into colour 'blocks,' as illustrated. Click **Commit** when you are happy with the result.

6   To close **PhotoLab** and return to the PagePlus workspace, click **OK**.

The **Median** filter is normally used to reduce 'noise' in an image.

7   On the Tools toolbar, select the **Quick Rectangle** and draw a small square on your page (ours was about 1.5 cm x 1.5 cm).

8   Select the shape, hold down the **Ctrl** key, and then drag to the right to create a copy.

9   Repeat the previous step to create five identical squares.

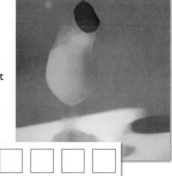

10 Select the first square, click the **Colour** tab, and then click the
✎ **Colour Picker**.

11 On the image, click and drag to select the first colour you want to add
to your new colour scheme.

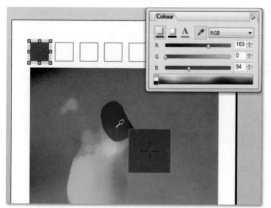

The popup colour
sample updates as
you drag to
different areas of
the image.

When you are
happy with the
colour displayed in
the sample, release
the mouse button.

The selected colour is applied to the square, and added to the
▦ **Publication Palette** on the
Swatches tab.

12 Selecting each of the remaining
squares in turn, repeat the previous
step to fill the shapes with four
additional colours from your image.

13 On the **Swatches** tab, scroll to the
end of the palette
swatches to find your new
custom colours displayed.

We're now ready to
create our new colour
scheme.

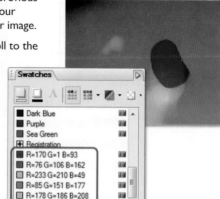

You don't have to use QuickShapes to display your selected colours, but we think it's useful to see the colour swatches next to each other and the image on the page.

This allows you to determine if the colours work together with the image, and when isolated from the image. You can quickly and easily adjust the colours, pick new ones, or change the colour order, before deciding on your final scheme colours.

We used five squares—one for each main scheme colour—but you can create more than this to begin with. Once you've filled your squares with a selection of colours you can then decide on your final palette.

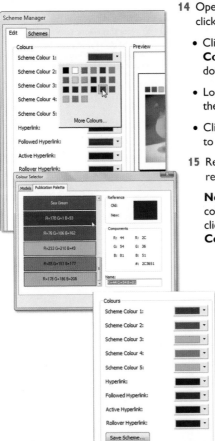

14 Open the **Scheme Manager** and click the **Edit** tab.

- Click the arrow next to **Scheme Colour 1** to expand the drop-down palette.

- Locate the colours you added in the previous steps.

- Click the colour you want to assign to **Scheme Colour 1**.

15 Repeat step 12 to assign the remaining scheme colours.

Note: If you don't see your colours in the drop-down palette, click **More Colours** to open the **Colour Selector** dialog.

On the **Publication Palette** tab, you will find the colours at the end of the palette list. Click the colour you want to assign to the scheme swatch, and then click **OK**.

16 Click **Save Scheme** and type a name for your colour scheme.

17 On the **Schemes** tab, scroll to find your new colour scheme.

18 Click the **Swatches** tab. Note that the swatches at the bottom of the tab now display your custom scheme colours.

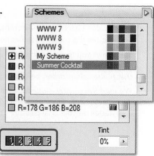

You can use these swatches to apply scheme colours to objects on your page.

Congratulations, you've created a custom colour scheme from scratch! It's a relatively simple process, but one which we hope you'll find useful in your future PagePlus publications.

Note that colour schemes are saved globally, so you'll be able to apply this scheme to your future PagePlus publications.

That concludes our tutorial. We've covered a lot of material here; we hope you've enjoyed working through the exercises. For more information about effective use of colour in design, see the tutorial *Designing With Colour*.

Have fun experimenting!

Tables

We show you how to create, edit and format tables by creating a price list for a three-fold flyer.

In this tutorial, we'll show you how to:

- Import a table.
- Add and delete rows and columns.
- Apply **Auto Format**.
- Customize an existing **Auto Format**.

Tables

Tables are a great way of displaying all forms of data quickly and easily. They can also be used as layout tools. Price lists, menus, general lists, school timetables, research data, opening times—all look best when inserted into a table on your publication. The best part is that PagePlus makes this easy to do.

In this tutorial, we are going to add a price list to the the back of a health spa flyer. We've included the document, **flyer2.ppp**, in the **...\Workspace\Table** folder.

In a typical installation, you will find this in:

C:\Program Files\Serif\PagePlus\X4\Tutorials

Let's get started.

To open the Workspace file

1 In the **Startup Wizard**, click **Open Saved Publication**.

2 Browse to the **flyer2.ppp** file, click to select it and then click **Open**.

   The publication opens in the PagePlus workspace.

3 On the **Pages** tab, double-click on the 'Back' page to display it.

We're ready to add our table.

To create a table

1 On the Tools toolbar, click the **Table Tool**.

2 Position your mouse pointer over the left margin guide, just below the logo banner. Click and drag to create a table between the margin guides.

3 In the **Create Table** dialog:

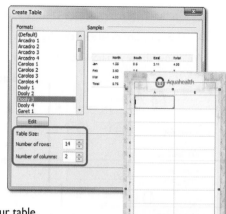

- In the **Format** list, click **Dooly 3**.

- Set the **Number of rows** to **14**.

- Set the **Number of columns** to **2**.

- Click **OK**.

The two column table is added to our page.

Let's now add the data to our table.

To add table data

1 Click in the first cell of the table and type the word 'Treatment'.

2 Click in the next header cell and type 'Price'.

3 Press the right arrow. Notice that the cursor goes to the next available cell. Type 'Aromatherapy', and press the right arrow to move to the next cell.

4 Type '£65'.

5 (Optional) Complete the table by adding the name and price of the other treatments found within the flyer.

Now that we've added all of the treatments, you'll notice that we have two rows left over. As they're not needed, we can delete them.

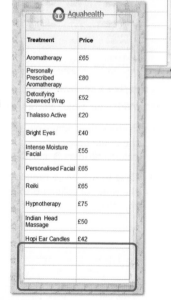

Treatment	Price
Aromatherapy	£65
Personally Prescribed Aromatherapy	£80
Detoxifying Seaweed Wrap	£52
Thalasso Active	£20
Bright Eyes	£40
Intense Moisture Facial	£55
Personalised Facial	£65
Reiki	£65
Hypnotherapy	£75
Indian Head Massage	£50
Hopi Ear Candles	£42

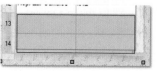

To delete a row

1 Click inside the first cell that you want to delete and then drag over the other three empty cells.

2 On the **Table** menu, click **Delete > Row(s)**.

3 The rows are deleted from the table.

We'll now show you how to add a column to your table.

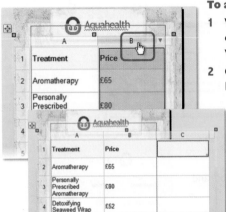

To add a column

1 With your table selected, click on the column header **B**. The whole column is highlighted.

2 On the **Table** menu, click **Insert > Columns**.

3 In the dialog, select the **After selected cells** option and click **OK**.

A new column is added to the right of the table.

To resize a column

1 With your table selected, click on the column header **B**.

2 Position the pointer on the divide between column headers **B** and **C**.

3 Drag to the left to reduce the width of column B so that the word 'Price' just fits.

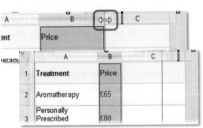

4 In the heading row of column C, type 'Duration'. Don't worry if the formatting is different, we'll fix this in a minute.

5 Click on column header **C** to select the column.

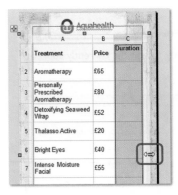

6 On the **Table** menu, click **Autofit to Contents > Column(s)**.

7 Finally, drag the centre handle of the table to the right so that it fits to the page margin again.

Now that the table fits nicely on the page, type the treatment duration in the new column that you created. You'll notice that the formatting is slightly different to that in the first two columns. We can fix this by re-applying the table **Auto Format**.

To apply table Auto Format

1 Click on the table to select it.

2 On the Table context toolbar, click ▦ **Auto Format**.

3 In the **AutoFormat** dialog, in the **Format** pane, click **Dooly 3** and then click **OK**.

The table format is reapplied.

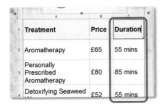

To create a custom table format

1   On the **Table** menu, click **Edit AutoFormat...**

The **Table Formats** dialog opens, ready to edit the currently applied table format.

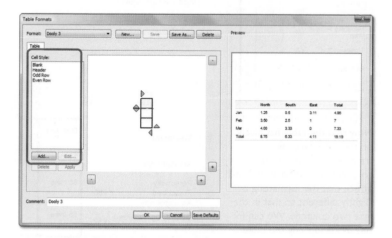

2   In the **Cell Style** pane, click **Odd Row** and then click **Edit...**

3   In the **Cell Properties** dialog:

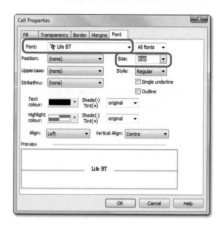

- Click the **Font** tab.

- In the **Font** drop-down list, select **Life BT**.

- In the **Size** drop-down list, select **9 pt**.

- Click **OK**.

4   In the **Cell Style** pane, click **Even Row** and then click **Edit...** and repeat step 3.

5   In the **Cell Style** pane, click **Header** and then click **Edit...**

6   In the **Cell Properties** dialog:

     • Click the **Font** tab.

     • In the **Font** drop-down list, select **Life BT**.

     • Click **OK**.

7   Click **Save As...**

8   Type a name for your new format, for example 'Flyer', and click **OK**.

9   Finally, click **OK** to close the **Table Formats** dialog.

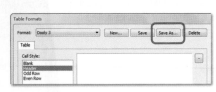

Your table is updated with the new format. By formatting the table in this way, you will be able to quickly apply this style to any table in future publications with the **Auto Format** button on the toolbar.

There are many more things that you can do with table formatting, for example, you can change cell colour to match your publication and create your own from scratch. You can also add inline images as in the product list example on the right.

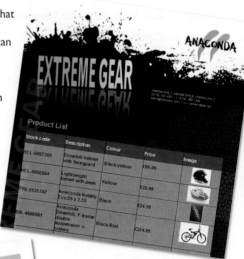

Why not create your own calendar with the 📅 **Calendar Tool**? The formatting techniques are very similar and a Wizard will guide you through the initial setup.

Although beyond the scope of this tutorial, you'll find more information in the online Help and on the **How To** tab. Have fun!

Design

These tutorials offer a wealth of information for PagePlus users of all abilities.

Whether you're creating a simple greetings card, a multi-page brochure or newsletter, or a business website, we'll show you how to create effective, eye-catching layouts, choose the right colours for your publication, and make the most of your images and photographs.

The focus here is on good desktop publishing practices to help you get the best out of your software, and produce publications you can be proud of.

Designing on a Grid

In this tutorial, we'll explore the design phase of document creation. With the grid as our layout guide, we'll look at the various ways that elements—text, images, graphic objects, and so on—can work together to produce effective layouts.

The grid provides a structured framework for a layout, but it should not limit design or stifle creativity. Rather than forcing you to work rigidly within its confines, the grid layout should work for you, allowing you to dictate the look and feel of your publication. We're confident you'll never look back!

In the following pages, we'll discuss:

- Basic grid structures
- Asymmetrical grids
- Margins and row and column gaps
- Mixed grids
- Breaking out of the grid
- Choosing the right grid for your publication

Designing on a Grid

Grid structures are vital to successful document design, and especially so for documents containing a mixture of text and graphics. If you don't believe us, examine a few of those magazines in your doctor's waiting room. Whatever the subject matter, and no matter how random the layout appears, the underlying structure will generally be based on a carefully designed grid.

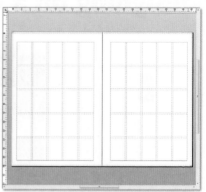

In the following pages, we'll look at some different grid structures and illustrate various layout options for each. Along the way, we'll offer tips and suggestions for creating successful grid-based layouts—we'll even encourage you to break the rules occasionally!

At the end of the tutorial, we'll provide some guidelines to help you choose the right grid for your particular project.

1: Basic grid structures

Let's start by looking at some basic grid structures.

Two-column grids

Two-column grids are mostly used in books, newsletters, or narrow publications where the column width is limited. Although this layout is very simple, you can still achieve variety by allowing some elements—for example, images and headlines—to span both columns on the page.

However, in wide publications, such as magazines or 'coffee table books,' the text columns in a two-column grid would generally be too wide for comfortable reading.

Three-column grids

These offer more flexibility than two-column grids because text and images can span one, two, or all of the columns. Three-column grids work for most layouts, even wide ones, and are particularly suited to publications that do not require complex arrangement of elements.

An alternative to the three-column grid is the three-row grid. This format is great for laying out narrow documents such as the tri-fold brochure.

Four- or more column grids

If you need to place a variety of elements into your layout—text, images, graphics, and so on—you'll find that grids with four or more columns offer the most flexibility.

Generally, grids with an uneven number of grid columns work best. Five- and even seven-column grids provide maximum flexibility and also allow for asymmetrical placement of elements, which tends to be more visually appealing than a symmetrical layout.

The examples on the right illustrate two different ways we can place the same information onto a seven-column grid.

Notice how we have created 'white space' by leaving some columns empty. Effective use of white space creates breathing space, especially on a busy page.

> ⚠️ **4-column grids**
>
> 4-column grids can be problematic because a single column is often too narrow for comfortable reading or for placing a graphic. Unless you are sure this structure will work for you, you could end up with most layout elements spanning two columns. In this case, the finished layout will appear to be based on two columns rather than four.

2: Asymmetrical grids

One of the most important features of the grid structure is its flexibility. So far, we've shown you how to add interest to your pages by leaving a column empty. In this section, we'll explore this idea further and show you how asymmetrical grids can liven up your layouts.

🔖 For instructions on setting up asymmetrical grids, see the *Creating Grid Layouts* tutorial.

Basic three-column grid

Our first example—a basic grid consisting of three equally sized columns—displays text columns and images in a pleasing, but conventional arrangement. Note that some elements span multiple columns.

Basic three-column grid

Image spanning three columns

Image spanning two columns

Text frame spanning two columns

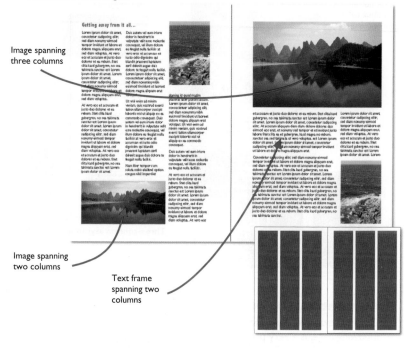

Three-column asymmetrical grid

In this example, we've dragged our column guides to make three columns of distinctly different sizes. To provide page-to-page consistency throughout our publication, we've created a 'mirrored' layout. Notice again that some elements span multiple columns, and that on the right page we have intentionally left the narrow centre column blank.

Narrow column used for pull quotes, or left blank to create white space.

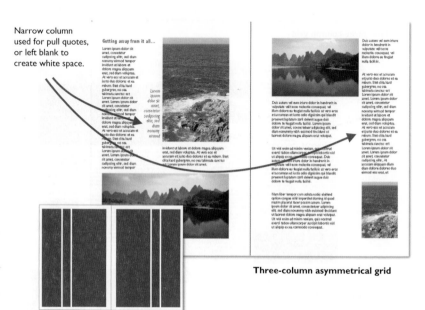

Three-column asymmetrical grid

Asymmetrical grid with sidebar

Our final example, illustrated on the following page, is a very popular asymmetrical layout. This grid makes use of a narrow side column, or 'sidebar,' which is not used for main body copy, but instead holds related text (headings, pull quotes, notes, and so on), graphics, or simply white space.

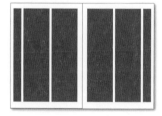

The following list describes some common uses of the sidebar:

- To display headings.

  Particularly useful in complex hierarchical documents, headings displayed in sidebar columns help to organize a document and allow the reader to quickly scan the page to find the information they are looking for.

- To bring the reader's attention to important information that you want to emphasize.

- To hold information that is relevant to the main subject of the body copy, but not part of the main text flow. For example, a note, suggestion, or warning.

- To declutter a complex layout by providing white space.

On the left page of our sample layout, below, the sidebar holds an initial adjacent cap and a note box. On the right page, the column is intentionally left blank; this balances the spread and creates an open and airy feel that complements the imagery perfectly.

Asymmetrical grid with sidebar

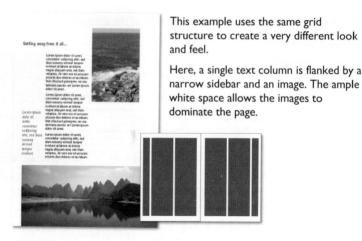

This example uses the same grid structure to create a very different look and feel.

Here, a single text column is flanked by a narrow sidebar and an image. The ample white space allows the images to dominate the page.

3: Margins and row and column gaps

Besides choosing the number, width, and arrangement of your columns, there are some other important grid elements that you must consider: page margins, and row and column gaps.

Page margins

No matter what type of document you're working on, it's rare that your page margins will all be of equal width. For example, you may want more space at the top or bottom of each page—for page header or page footer information, page numbers, and so on.

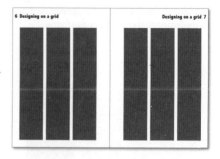

For bound publications, you'll usually find that the inside margins are considerably wider than the outside margins. This prevents text and images that are placed in the centre of a spread from 'disappearing' into the spine.

💡 If your document is to be printed professionally, avoid last-minute problems by discussing margins and gutter widths with your printer—*before* you start creating your layout.

Row and column gaps

Row and column gaps are the spaces between the rows and columns in a grid structure.

There are no strict rules about the width of these spaces, but if you make them too narrow your text columns will be difficult to read. We suggest that you experiment to find the gap width that works best for your particular layout.

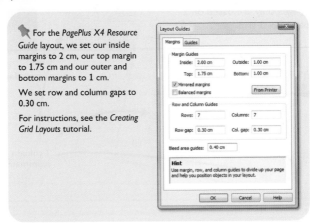

For the *PagePlus X4 Resource Guide* layout, we set our inside margins to 2 cm, our top margin to 1.75 cm and our outer and bottom margins to 1 cm.

We set row and column gaps to 0.30 cm.

For instructions, see the *Creating Grid Layouts* tutorial.

4: Mixed grid layouts

We've stressed the importance of using a grid to maintain page-to-page consistency throughout a document. However, if certain pages present information that varies greatly from the rest of the document, don't try to force them to conform to a structure that doesn't really suit the purpose. Instead, simply use a different grid for these pages.

Let's suppose we're creating a brochure that contains lots of text, and some images that we want to present all together on one or two pages. For this project, it makes sense to use one grid for the text-heavy pages and another for displaying the images.

In our example, the main pages are based on an asymmetrical three-column grid—two wide columns for the main text flow and a narrow sidebar for headings, pull quotes and selected images. Pages displaying images only are based on a basic 3 x 3 grid.

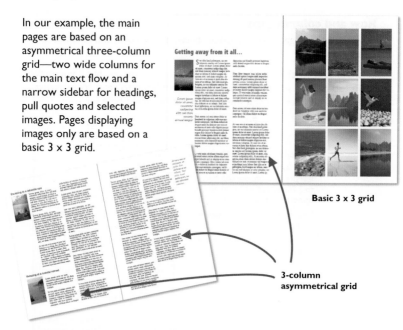

Basic 3 x 3 grid

3-column asymmetrical grid

5: Breaking out of the grid

We've convinced you (we hope!) of the power and flexibility of the grid. Now, we'll encourage you to break the rules and occasionally break out of the grid.

Example 1

Add impact and visual interest to a layout by extending an element out to the page edge.

This works especially well for presenting large images (we've used this technique in many of the PagePlus tutorials!).

Example 2

Try positioning some elements outside of the grid. On the right page of the newsletter spread below, see how the text frame containing the pull quote is centred on the page, breaking the underlying three-column grid structure.

Example 3

If you're feeling adventurous, why not break the grid by rotating some layout objects. Be careful not to overdo this one though, and make sure that other elements remain within the grid, or your page will appear disorganized.

Example 4

Diagonal lines can add interest to a grid layout. In this example, we've cut through our columns, but have still aligned the image with the grid.

6: Choosing the right grid

When planning your layout, you need to have a clear idea of what your finished document should look like, what format is required, the purpose of the document, who will be reading it, how it will be printed, and so on. Once you've answered these questions, you'll have a better understanding of the type of grid structure required. The following guidelines should help you choose and plan your grid layout.

Content

The most important question to ask yourself is this: "Is the document predominantly text or images?" For lots of text with few images, try a simple two- or three-column grid.

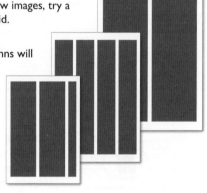

For lots of graphics, photos, or illustrations, four or more columns will give you more scope to place and size these elements.

Do you want to include notes, pull quotes, or other accent information? Is the document hierarchical, with lots of headings and subheadings? If so, consider an asymmetrical grid with a sidebar column.

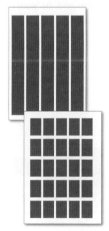

Complexity

For complex documents—for example, a newsletter containing a mix of text and graphics—grids with more columns and/or rows provide more design options. However, avoid making the grid too complex or you'll lose sight of the underlying structure.

Document type

Newsletters usually contain more text so simple column-based layouts tend to work best. For more sophisticated publications, such as illustrated books, more columns will provide more design options. Publications with mainly small articles and graphics— a sales brochure or catalogue, for example—are more suited to grids containing both columns and rows.

Design tips

- Don't confine page elements to individual grid units. In grids with four or more columns, text and images can span several grid units.

- Leave some grid units empty, or use them for accents such as small photos, adjacent caps, headlines, and so on.

- Use your gutters and margins. Extending some images and headlines into the bleed area can add interest to a layout.

Summary

In this tutorial, our main objective was to illustrate the power and flexibility of the grid, and explain why it is such an important document design tool. We hope that we've achieved this objective.

To quickly get started with grids, we've included some samples in the **...\Workspace\Grid Layouts** folder of your PagePlus installation directory.

In a standard installation, you'll find this folder in the following location:

C:\Program Files\Serif\PagePlus\X4\Tutorials

For step-by-step instructions on setting up a grid structure from scratch, see the *Creating Grid Layouts* tutorial.

Creating Grid Layouts

Effective document design depends on a clear visual structure that conveys and complements the main message. The right layout should provide a consistent framework to help you organize the various elements of your pages, but should also be flexible enough to let you exercise your creativity.

In the previous tutorial, *Designing on a Grid*, we explored the various ways that layout elements can be placed together on an underlying invisible grid structure.

In this tutorial, we will continue with this theme and show you how to set up a basic grid for a multi-column layout.

You'll learn how to:

- Use the **Page Setup** dialog to set up your page size and type.
- Use the **Layout Guides** dialog to set up margins, columns, rows, and bleed area guides.
- Work with ruler guides.
- Create asymmetrical grids.
- View and customize the dot grid.

Creating Grid Layouts

The grid is a traditional layout tool that dates back to the days when text was typeset onto vertical strips of paper, which were then manually cut and pasted onto card sheets. The print production process has changed dramatically since then, but the grid is still a popular page layout tool because it provides some crucial functions—for both reader and designer.

When reading any type of document, we expect a certain consistency from page to page. For example, we expect to find page numbers, footnotes, sidebar text, and so on, in the same place on each page. When all the text and design elements in a document have a consistent look and feel, readability is significantly enhanced.

A grid structure—such as the one illustrated here (used for this document)—makes it easier to provide this consistency by helping to determine such things as the width of text columns, the space around images and graphic objects, the placement of repeating elements throughout a publication, and so on. As you work with the grid, you'll find that having these guidelines for object placement significantly speeds up

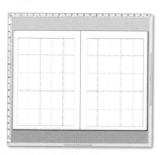

the layout process, and helps to ensure that your final layout will be a success.

In this tutorial, we'll introduce you to the various elements of the grid, and show you how to set up a basic grid structure in PagePlus.

Using grid templates

If you want to use a grid, but don't want to create one from scratch, you can quickly get started with one of our ready-made grid templates. In a standard installation, you'll find these in the **...\Workspace\Grid Layouts** folder in the following location:

C:\Program Files\Serif\PagePlus\X4\Tutorials

You can use the templates 'as is,' or customize them to suit your needs using the procedures outlined in the following sections.

I: Setting up the page

Our first task is to create a new document and set up our page size and type.

To set up the page

1   On the **File** menu, select **New**, then click **New from Startup Wizard**.

In the Startup Wizard, click **Start New Publication**, choose **A4** or **Letter** size paper, and click **OK**.

Let's add two pages to this publication.

2   In the Hintline toolbar, click the **Page Manager** (or click **Insert**, then **Page**).

3   In the **Page Manager** dialog, on the **Insert** tab:

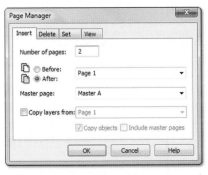

* In the **Number of pages** box, type **2**.

  Notice that we can also select *where* to add our pages. For example, if this were a multi-page document, we could select **Before** or **After**, and then choose the page number from the drop-down list.

* We just have one page, so accept the default values (**After**, **Page** 1). Click **OK**.

The Hintline toolbar now displays '2 of 3,' indicating that you are currently working on page 2 of a 3 page document.

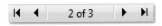

4 On the **File** menu, click **Page Setup**. In the **Page Setup** dialog:

- To set up the page layout as facing pages (also known as spreads), select the **Facing pages** check box.

- To set up dual master pages (allowing you to run elements across the spread in the background of the publication, or position left- and right-side page numbers), select the **Dual master pages** check box.

- Click **OK**.

If you're setting up a facing-page layout where both left and right pages share the same master page, and you don't need to run background elements across the spread, clear the **Dual master pages** check box.

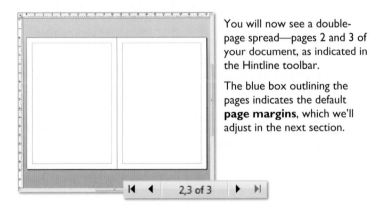

You will now see a double-page spread—pages 2 and 3 of your document, as indicated in the Hintline toolbar.

The blue box outlining the pages indicates the default **page margins**, which we'll adjust in the next section.

2: Setting up layout guides

Layout guides are visual guide lines that help you position layout elements, either 'by eye' or with snapping turned on (you'll find the 🔲 ▾ **Snapping** button at the right of the Hintline toolbar). Layout guides include page margins, row and column guides, and bleed area guides. In PagePlus, margins are shown as solid blue lines; row, column, and bleed area guides are shown as dashed blue lines.

To set up layout guides

1   Click on a blank area of the page and then on the Page context toolbar, click 🔲 Layout Guides . (You can also click **File**, then **Layout Guides**, or right-click on a blank area of the page and choose **Layout Guides**.)

In the **Layout Guides** dialog, in the **Margin Guides** section:

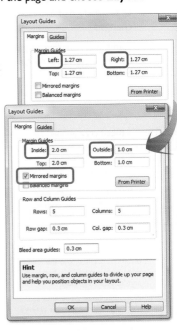

*   Select the **Mirrored margins** check box.

    This tells PagePlus to change the **Left** margin setting to the 'Inside' margin on both facing pages, and to change the **Right** margin to the 'Outside' margin on both pages.

*   Set the **Inside page margin to 2.00** cm.

*   Set the **Outside page margin** to **1.00** cm.

*   Set the **Top page** margin to **2.00** cm.

*   Set the **Bottom page** margin to **1.00** cm.

2   In the **Row and Column Guides** section:

*   Set the number of **Rows to 5**.

*   Set the number of **Columns to 5**.

*   Set the **Row gap** (the space between your rows) to **0.30** cm.

- Set the **Column gap** (the space between your columns) to **0.30** cm.

- Set the **Bleed area guides** (the 'trim edge' of the page) to **0.30** cm.

3 Click **OK**.

You should now see a 5 × 5 blue grid superimposed on each of your pages. Note also that the position of the margins has changed.

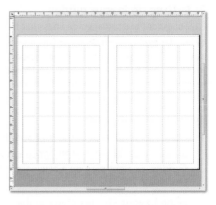

Can't see your layout guides? On the **View** menu, ensure that **Guide Lines** and **Bleed Area Guides** are selected, and that **Trimmed Mode** is not selected.

 Bleed area guides

These guides help you to position 'bleed elements' that you want to run to the edge of a page. If your document is to be professionally printed, we suggest that you allow for inaccuracies in the trimming process by extending any bleed elements beyond the trim edge.

The page border expands by the distance specified, and the trim edge is shown with dashed lines and 'scissors' symbols.

Note that these guide lines are *visual aids* only; the **Print** dialog's **Bleed limit** setting extends the *actual* output page size.

See *Setting prepress options* in the *Generating professional output* online Help topic.

3: Adding ruler guides

You can set up horizontal and vertical 'snap-to' ruler guides—non-printing, solid red lines that you can use to align headlines, pictures, and other layout elements.

There are two ways to create ruler guides:

- Automatically—in the **Layout Guides** dialog, on the **Guides** tab. Use this method to place multiple ruler guides onto a page in precise positions.

  - or -

- Manually—by clicking and dragging on the rulers. Use this method to place individual ruler guides onto a page as you work.

To create a ruler guide automatically

1 Click on a blank area of the page and then on the Page context bar, click 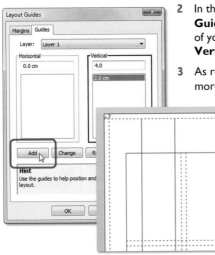 Layout Guides .

2 In the **Layout Guides** dialog, on the **Guides** tab, type the desired position of your guide into the **Horizontal** or **Vertical** box. Click **Add**.

3 As required, repeat step 2 to add more guides, and then click **OK**.

Solid red lines now indicate the ruler guides you created.

To create a guide manually

• Click and drag on the horizontal or vertical ruler.

A red line indicates the new ruler guide.

If you now open the **Layout Guides** dialog and view the **Guides** tab, you'll see that your guide has been added to the list.

The dialog on the right shows the guides we created to position the page headers and numbers in our publication.

If a text object is selected, clicking within the object's ruler region adds a tab stop; clicking and dragging elsewhere on the ruler creates a ruler guide.

Moving and deleting ruler guides

Whichever method you use to create your ruler guides, you can move
them around or delete them at any time.

To move a ruler guide

• Click and drag the red guide line.

  As you drag, the solid line changes to
  a dashed line; once positioned, the
  line again becomes solid.

To delete a ruler guide

• In the **Layout Guides** dialog: On the
  Guides tab, select the guide and click
  Remove (to delete all ruler guides,
  click **Remove All**.)

  - or -

• On the page: Drag and drop the red
  guide line anywhere outside the page
  area.

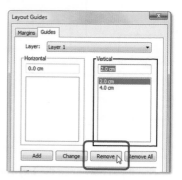

 Locking and resetting your guide lines

To prevent your margins, columns, rows, and ruler guides from accidentally being moved,
you can lock them.

To lock your guides:

1 On the **Tools** menu, click **Options**.

2 In the left **Options** list, expand the **Layout** category and click **Display**.

3 Select the **Lock guide lines** check box and click **OK**.

Note that this option will also lock the red ruler guides, so you will not be able to drag
them freely around your page.

If you choose not to lock your guidelines, you can still easily reset your original layout.

To reset your layout

• Click **File > Layout Guides**, click the **Margins** tab, and then click **OK**.

4: Creating asymmetrical grids

Once you've set up your basic row and column guides, you can manually adjust them to make your layouts even more flexible. This feature is particularly useful for setting up asymmetrical grid layouts, such as the three-column layout illustrated here.

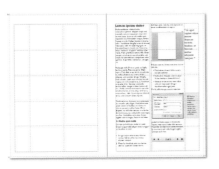

(In order to move the row and column guides, you must clear the **Lock guide lines** option in the **Options** dialog.)

To adjust custom rows and columns

- Click and drag a dashed blue row or column guide line.

You will have to adjust the row and column guides on each page of your document.

5: Asymmetrical grids on multi-page documents

When working on multi-page documents, rather than manually adjusting the row and column guides on each page of your document, there are various ways to speed up the process.

Note: For each of the following methods, you'll first need to make sure that the **Facing pages** and **Dual master pages** options are selected in the **Page Setup** dialog.

Asymmetrical grid: Method 1

1 In **Normal** page view, open the **Layout Guides** dialog.

   On the **Margins** tab, set up the basic number of grid units for your publication.

2 In **Master Page** view, add ruler guides to mark the asymmetrical units. You can set these up manually or automatically, as you prefer (see section 3, *Adding ruler guides*).

These guides will be visible on all pages of the publication.

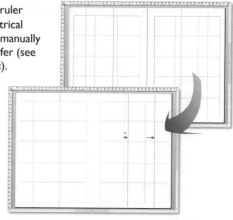

3 In **Normal** page view, drag the row and column guides onto the ruler guides as you work on each page. You'll need to zoom in quite a lot to achieve precise guide placement. As the guides line up exactly, you may find that your ruler guide disappears underneath the layout guide.

Asymmetrical grid: Method 2

1 In **Normal** page view, open the **Layout Guides** dialog. On the **Margins** tab, set up a basic grid comprising a few more grid units than you need.

For example, to end up with a three-column asymmetrical grid, try starting with a basic five- or six-column grid.

In our illustration we used a basic seven-column grid as the starting point for a four-column asymmetrical layout.

You may need to experiment with this to get it right.

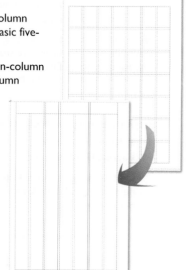

2 In **Master Page** view, use ruler guides to mark the asymmetrical grid units. You can set these up manually or automatically, as you prefer (see section 3, *Adding ruler guides*).

These guides will be visible on all pages of the publication.

3 When you've added all of your ruler guides, you can remove the original row and column guides.

To do this, simply open the **Layout Guides** dialog and type the number '1' in the **Rows** and **Columns** boxes. Click **OK**.

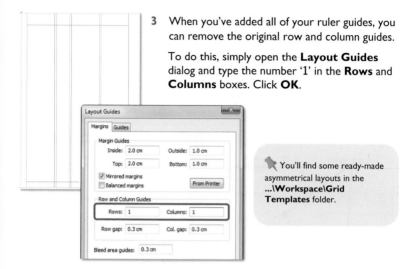

You'll find some ready-made asymmetrical layouts in the **...\Workspace\Grid Templates** folder.

Asymmetrical grid: Method 3

1 In **Normal** page view, in the **Layout Guides** dialog, set up a one row, one column grid.

2 In **Master Page** view, set up your asymmetrical grid using only the red ruler guides. You can set these up manually or automatically, as you prefer (see section 3, *Adding ruler guides*).

These guides will be visible on all pages of the publication.

6: Using the dot grid

PagePlus provides an optional dot grid, which you can use for precise placement of layout elements. If required, you can customize the dot grid—for example, by changing the grid display type and colour.

To display or hide the dot grid

• On the **View** menu, click **Dot Grid**.

To customize the dot grid

1 On the **Tools** menu, click **Options**.

2 In the left **Options** list, expand the Layout category and click **Snapping**.

3 Select the **Dot Grid** check box.

Subdivisions

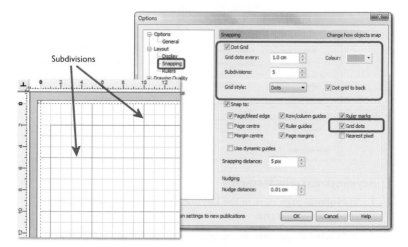

4 Make the following changes as required:

- In the **Grid dots every** box, choose the dot grid spacing.

- To highlight certain lines, set the **Subdivisions**. In our example, every fifth line is highlighted.

- In the **Grid style** drop-down list, choose the grid display type.

  For example, to create the graph-paper effect shown here, choose **Solid**.

- In the **Colour** box, click to select a new grid colour from the drop-down palette. If you are using subdivisions, mid to light greys produce the clearest display.

- If you want your layout elements to snap to the dot grid, in the **Snap to** section, select the **Grid dots** option.

- Check the **Dot grid to back** option if you want the grid to appear behind the objects on the page.

What's next?

If you've followed the steps of this tutorial, you should now know how to set up a grid layout for any type of publication.

When you are happy with your layout, you can start placing your text and graphics elements onto it. If you need help with this, refer back to the previous tutorial, *Designing on a Grid*, for some layout ideas.

Creative Cropping

Whether you're using PagePlus to create a newsletter, brochure, website, or even a simple greetings card, chances are that at some point you'll be working with images.

In this tutorial, we'll show you how effective image cropping can improve a layout by creating a focal point, emphasizing a concept, removing unwanted elements, or simply adding drama to your pages.

You'll learn how to:

- Apply the Rule of Thirds.
- Make small spaces work for you.
- Use zoom and 'extreme cropping' techniques.
- Make the most of the white space on your page.
- Isolate sections of an image to create variety.
- Crop away the boring bits!

Creative Cropping

You may have found the perfect photo for your paper publication or your website, but that doesn't mean that you can't improve it. Every image has boundaries, and you can decide where those boundaries should be. In the following pages, we'll illustrate some effective and powerful cropping techniques that are sure to improve your layouts. Try them with your own photos—you'll be surprised what a difference they can make.

1: Apply the Rule of Thirds

The photographer's favourite, this rule states that if you divide your image roughly into thirds, horizontally and vertically, any point(s) where those lines intersect is a good place to position your main subject. Your chosen image may not conform to this standard, but you can correct this with some creative cropping.

For example, we've cropped this image so that our subject is positioned roughly at the one-third point. We've focused in on the runner and kept enough of the background to provide context.

Notice also that although we have cropped away the lower and upper portions of the subject, we have still maintained the essence of the image.

2: Make the most of small spaces

Small layouts can be problematic, and especially when you want to include an image. Many people make the mistake of simply resizing their image to fit into the space, which usually reduces the impact and results in a weak composition. Instead, crop your image effectively and make that small space work for you! Let's look at two common 'small space' design challenges: web banners and business cards.

Website banner

Here, the challenge lay in conveying the message of the site in a very shallow space.

To solve the problem, we looked for a photo that we could 'slice,' while still presenting enough information to get the message across.

Business card

Here, you might be tempted to use the whole image, simply resizing it to fit the dimensions of the business card.

However, by zooming into a section of the image, we've given our design much more impact and have opened up a space to position our text elements.

3: Zoom in

Zooming closely into a subject and then using extreme cropping can strengthen a focal point and add to the drama in an image.

In our first example, we zoomed in closely and cropped away everything but the subjects. By doing so, we heightened the drama in an already dynamic image.

You can use this technique on many different types of images, but it's especially effective for portraits. When cropping portrait photos, aim to crop at eye-level, which is about two-fifths of the way down the page.

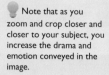

💡 Note that as you zoom and crop closer and closer to your subject, you increase the drama and emotion conveyed in the image.

4: Isolate sections of an image

Isolating different sections of an image or images can be a great way to create variety and add 'movement' to your page. You can also use this technique to convey different stories from the same image.

Wedding album

In this example, we've contrasted a single vertical slice with a rectangular crop of the wedding bouquet.

Our wedding

In this example, we cropped vertical slices from three photos to create an interesting wedding album cover.

This composition works particularly well because the three images share similar coloration.

Slicing the images into narrow columns creates movement and moves the eye down the page.

Our wedding

 Using white space

In both examples, notice how we have made use of white space by reducing the size of our composition relative to the page. This effectively 'disconnects' the image from the page edge so it appears to be borderless.

In the first example, rather than centring the subject vertically on the page, we have raised it to give three different margin widths. This again helps to eliminate the border effect.

Flyer

Here, we've cropped sections from the same image to create an interesting montage effect for a coffee shop flyer.

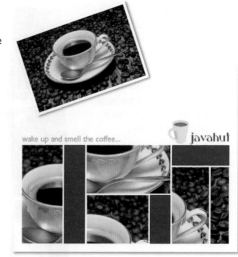

For the solid blocks of colour and the text, we used the ✏ **Colour Picker** tool (on the **Colour** tab) to sample colours directly from our image.

To learn more about this technique, see the *Colour Schemes* and *Designing with Colour* tutorials.

The same effect would work equally well on a website or brochure, or even as the cover of family photo album...

💡 Using different zoom levels creates contrast and variety, adding interest to the page.

5: Crop away the boring bits!

We couldn't end this tutorial without stressing the most important cropping tip: get rid of the boring stuff!

Unless you're a professional photographer, you'll usually find that even your best planned photos contain elements that you don't want. Be strict with yourself and crop away anything that doesn't contribute to the image—we guarantee you'll be much happier with the results.

Designing With Colour

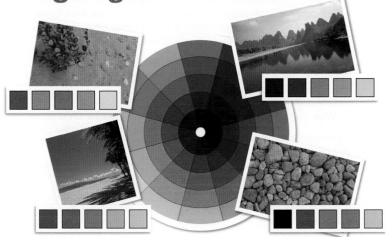

When designing your publications, one of the most important factors to consider is colour. Choose wisely and you'll attract the attention of your target audience, set the appropriate mood, and send the right message. Choose unwisely and you'll turn readers away—no matter how professional your layout or how interesting your content.

But how do you select a colour palette that's right for your publication? In this tutorial, we'll demystify the process and show you a few different ways to find the perfect colour for your projects.

You'll learn how to:

- Create a colour scheme from a photograph.
- Use colour theory to create a range of palettes.

Designing With Colour

While the use of colour is quite personal, our aim is to help you choose colours that are not only visually pleasing but also reflect the content of your publication.

Choosing colours

Designers use many different methods to choose colours for their documents and websites. In the following example, we have based our colour scheme on an image that we want to use on the front cover of a brochure. As mentioned previously, you might also take colours from a company logo or some other 'signature' image.

Alternatively, you could use an image that does not appear in your document, but which contains a range of colours you find particularly attractive and which portrays the mood and message you want your publication, or Web site, to convey to your audience.

If you want a more structured approach, you can even employ a little basic colour theory! A quick Internet search will provide you with lots of information on this subject—try searching on "use of colour in print (or Web) design" for example.

Don't underestimate the importance of colour choice when designing your PagePlus document or website.

No matter how professional your layout or how interesting your content, incorrect use of colour can result in pages that are ugly and/or difficult to read.

In this section, we'll step you through the following approaches:

Example 1: Find an image or photograph that portrays the mood or message of the document or site—this may not necessarily be related to the content—then choose a range of colours from the image.

Example 2: Choose a 'base' colour (you can take this from an image that will feature in your publication), then use colour theory to find colours that harmonize with it.

Example 1: Using an image or photograph

Suppose we're creating a brochure for a health spa. The first thing we need to do is think about the image we want to portray. We associate health spas with calmness and tranquility—it makes sense, therefore, not to use harsh or vibrant colours in our layouts.

1   Choose a few images that suit the mood. You could use a photograph, or an image found on the Internet or in a book or magazine (you'll need to scan the image so that you can open it on your computer).

The colour palettes of the following photographs all reflect the mood we want our brochure to convey.

Looking at these images, it's obvious that they fall into two distinct groups: one group contains various shades of blue along with natural and more muted tones; in the other group, softer earth tones predominate.

2   At this point, you (or your client) must decide which colour palette to use. For this tutorial, we'll assume that our health spa client prefers the muted tones of the 'pebbles' close-up photo.

3   You can now follow the procedure outlined in the *Colour Schemes* tutorial to create your custom colour scheme (see *Creating custom colour schemes from scratch*).

We suggest you start by creating lots of squares and fill them with a range of colours from the image.

When you have a good selection from which to choose, play around with the swatches and try different groupings before settling on your final five scheme colours.

4   If the choice is not obvious to you, create several different schemes using variations of your colour swatches. You can then switch between schemes to see how the look and feel of the publication changes.

💡 Can't decide which colour palette to use? It's a good idea to create a PagePlus colour scheme for each palette, and then 'mock up' a page using each scheme.

You might also do this if you're designing a document for a client and want to present them with a few options from which to choose.

Example 2: Using colour theory

This method starts with the selection of a 'base' colour. You can choose any colour you prefer.

In our example, we'll take our base colour from a photograph that will feature on the front cover of a 'Kids' Camp' brochure

1   Follow the procedure outlined in the *Colour Schemes* tutorial to extract a wide range of colours from your image.

   - Don't forget to add the **Median** adjustment first in **PhotoLab**, to create blocks of colour to work with.

   - Start with the 'big' colours. These are the ones you see first when you glance at the image: skin, hair, and shirt. Then extract the 'small' colours—mouth, eyes, highlights and shadows.

   - You need a good range of colours, but don't overdo it or you'll find it difficult to make your selection. You might only extract eight or ten colours, or you might find you need more. The exact number will vary depending on your image.

2   Group your results by colour, then sort each colour group by value from dark to light, deleting any colours that are too similar.

3   Select any one of your colours as your 'base.' Locate the colour on the colour wheel to determine whether it is warm or cool, and to see its relationship to other colours.

   - Our **warm colours** are found in the red areas of girl's shirt, and in her hair and skin tones. Choose from these colours if your aim is to give a softer, gentler look and feel to your publication.

   - Our **cool colours** are derived from the blue and white areas of the shirt, and from the eyes. These colours are generally used when a more serious or business-like approach is required.

4 Using your base colour and its position on the colour wheel, you can now start to create a range of colour palettes. There are several approaches you can take, including:

- Analogous

- Monochromatic

- Complement

- Split complement

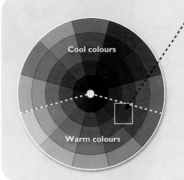

The Colour Wheel

The colour wheel is a basic model. It is meant as a guide only, so don't worry if you can't find an exact match for your colour.

Once you've located your base colour you can see its relationship to other colours and can then create a range of colour palettes that will work for your website.

Analogous colour palettes

Analogous colours are extracted from the two sections that sit either side of the base colour section.

These colours all share the same undertone—in our example, red-orange, red, and red-purple.

Analogous colour combinations are great for print or Web design as they are harmonious and very easy to work with.

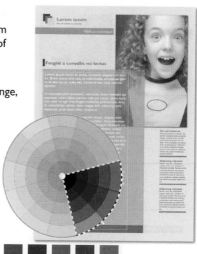

Monochromatic colour palettes

Monochromatic palettes consist of the dark, medium, and light values (the shades and tints) of your base colour.

You can choose your colour swatch values from the PagePlus palette, and then further increase the contrast by adjusting the **Tint** value on the **Swatches** tab.

- A shade is made by adding black to a colour to darken it.

- A tint is made by adding white to a colour to lighten it.

Complement colour palettes

You'll find the complement colours directly opposite the base colour range. Generally, the complement (in our case, the green range) is used as an accent.

These palettes provide extreme contrast, conveying energy and excitement. While often used in printed media, you should be wary of using this palette in Web design as such highly contrasted colours tend to be jarring to the eye when viewed on screen.

Split complement colour palettes

The split complement colours are the analogous colours of the complement itself.

Less jarring than the complement, this combination provides a more subtle contrast and a more harmonious palette.

In this example, the base colour red would be used as the accent colour in our design layout.

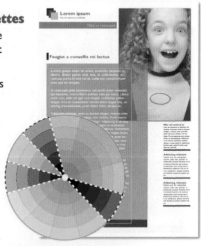

Mixing palettes

If you're feeling adventurous, you can also combine palettes to create some interesting effects.

For example, try contrasting your **base** colour and its **analogous** colours with the **complement**.

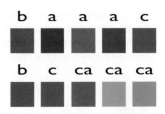

Alternatively, you could combine your **base** colour and its **complement** with the **complement's analogous** colours.

As you can see from our illustrations, each palette creates quite a different effect when applied to the same layout. Which one you choose depends on the message you want your publication to convey to your audience.

Accessibility

When choosing your colour schemes, it is worth bearing in mind that a small percentage of the population cannot differentiate between certain colours (the most common being red and green). To illustrate this, here are a few examples of the colour wheel when viewed by someone with one of the three main forms of colour blindness, protanope, deuteranope, and the rare tritanope:

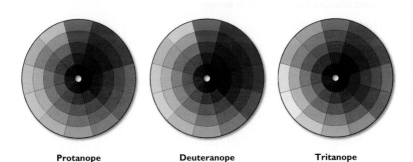

| **Protanope** | **Deuteranope** | **Tritanope** |

There is an excellent website called Vischeck that explains colour blindness in more detail. It also has a free plugin available for download that allows you to test your own site (or a screenshot of printed material) for colour use. The plugin works with Serif PhotoPlus and was used to create the images found within the *Accessibilty* section of this tutorial.

Visit the site at http://www.vischeck.com/

The following sample image serves well to illustrate the care needed when deciding on colour schemes. This example simulates deuteranope colour blindness, the most common of the three types mentioned here. Notice how the browns and the reds appear almost identical.

That concludes our tutorial. We've covered a lot of material here; we hope you've enjoyed working through the exercises and have learned something along the way. You should now be feeling comfortable creating your own colour schemes from scratch, and understand a little more about effective use of colour in design.

Have fun experimenting!

Designing a Logo

Learn all about logos, branding, and identity as we show you the secrets of effective logo design.

In this tutorial, we'll design logos suitable for business cards and other publications.

You'll learn how to:

- Use artistic text and graphics objects to design a logo.
- Use a variety of typefaces to create different effects.
- Use colour effectively in a layout.
- Position and align text and graphics objects.
- Group related objects together.

Designing a Logo

You may have noticed that some logos look better than others. Why is this? Is it the layout, the colours, the typeface, or a combination of all of these elements? Great designs are not a mystery and you don't need professional graphic design skills. By following some simple rules, you can ensure that your logo looks professional and conveys the right image.

In this exercise, we'll create a logo for a fictitious recruitment company. We'll demonstrate five different logo designs and explain how the elements in each of them work together to convey a different image.

In the following section, we'll show you the different techniques we used to create our five sample logos. We'll discuss the effectiveness of each, and give you some design tips to help you create your own.

Example 1

In our first example, we used a modern font in two different sizes and colours.

We expanded the text spacing and incorporated 'sunrise-coloured' graphic bars to give the impression of horizontal width—playing on the word 'horizon.' Let's break this down so you can see exactly how the effect was achieved.

H O R I Z O N **I** R E C R U I T M E N T

To create and format artistic text

1 On the Tools toolbar, click the A **Artistic Text Tool**.

2 Click anywhere in the document and type

   'HORIZON I RECRUITMENT.'

   Note that we've typed a letter 'I'   HORIZON I RECRUITMENT
   between the two words, leaving a
   space on either side.

A **logo** is a unique name, symbol, or trademark of a company or organization. Well-designed logos provide brand name recognition and promote a business presence. They achieve this because people process an image in their mind more easily than words. In addition, visual stimulation produces a more effective and long-lasting impact on the audience's memory than words alone.

3   Click in the line of text and press **Ctrl+A** to select both words.

4   Use the Text context toolbar, or the **Fonts** tab, to choose a sans serif font style for your text.

HORIZON I RECRUITMENT

5   In the text frame, double-click the word 'HORIZON' to highlight it,

HORIZON I RECRUITMENT

then on the **Character** tab, change the ⊤ **Font size** to 18 pt.

6   Repeat step 5 to change the size of the letter 'I' to 24 pt, and the size of the word 'RECRUITMENT' to 12.5 pt.

7   Click in the line of text and press **Ctrl+A** to select both words.

8   On the **Character** tab, change the A̅V̅ **Spacing** to a value of 10 pt.

By making these minor adjustments to font size and spacing, we have already created the impression of horizontal width and given a much more modern look and feel to the line of text.

H O R I Z O N   I   R E C R U I T M E N T

Let's change the text colour of the word 'RECRUITMENT.' This is a quick and easy way to create visual interest and contrast in a layout.

To change font colour

1   In the text frame, click and drag to highlight the letter 'I' and word 'RECRUITMENT.'

2   On the **Swatches** tab, click the A̲ **Text colour** and choose a palette from the ▦ **Palette** flyout. (We chose **Candy**.)

3   Select a dark blue-grey swatch and click to apply the colour.

C=88 M=56 Y=0 K=0

H O R I Z O N   I   R E C R U I T M E N T

Design Tip

Contrast is an important consideration when designing any publication layout. The simplest and most obvious contrast is black text on a white background, but you can be more adventurous and use opposite colours on the colour wheel—such colour pairs (e.g. red and green, blue and orange) are actually termed 'contrasting colours.' You'll find information to help you choose the right colours for your publication in the *Designing With Colour* tutorial.

Now to introduce a graphic element to our design. In the following section, we'll show you how to create the coloured bars using a basic Quick Shape. You'll be working at quite a detailed level, so it's a good idea to click to zoom in at this point.

To create and format a Quick Shape

1 Click the ⬜ ▾ **Quick Shape** button on the Tools toolbar and select the **Quick Rectangle** from the flyout.

2 Click and drag to create a rectangle under the first two letters of 'HORIZON.'

3 Select the rectangle, then on the **Swatches** tab, click the ▦ ▾ **Palette** drop-down list and select the **Standard RGB** palette.

4 Click the ▣ **Fill** button and select the pink (RGB 255, 95, 255) swatch.

5 With the rectangle still selected, click the ▣ **Line** button and select **None** or ▣.

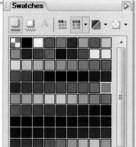

Now that we've created the template for our shape, we can copy and paste it to quickly create another three identical shapes.

To copy and paste an object

1 Select the object, right-click, and then click **Copy**.

2 Right-click again and click **Paste**.

3 Repeat steps 1 and 2 to create four identical shapes. PagePlus pastes the copies one on top of the other.

4 Click on each of the copies in turn and position them so that they span the word 'HORIZON.' Don't worry about spacing them exactly—we can use PagePlus alignment tools to do this.

To align objects on a page

1 Press and hold down the **Shift** key, then use the ⬆ **Pointer Tool** to click on each of the four bars. A blue bounding box appears around the group of objects.

2 On the **Align** tab click ▣ **Top** and ⫿⫿ **Space Evenly Across** relative to **Selection**.

The bars are now perfectly spaced and aligned. Let's go ahead and change their colours.

To change the colour of an object

1 Click to select the object—in this case the second bar on the left.

2 Click the **Swatches** tab, click the ⬜ **Fill** button, and then click one of the pale green colour swatches. We used RGB (188, 252, 184).

3 Repeat steps 1 and 2 to colour the other two bars. We used RGB (252, 136, 32)—orange, and RGB (0, 132, 132)—dark green.

H O R I Z O N | R E C R U I T M E N T

Congratulations, you've just created a simple, but effective company logo. As you can see, it doesn't require complicated procedures, or professional design skills. In fact, the simplest designs often work the best.

To further demonstrate this point, we'll show you a few more examples, all of which use simple techniques that you can adapt to suit your own needs.

Example 2

In this example, we used a fluid modern font (with slightly expanded text spacing) for the main company name 'Horizon,' contrasting it with a simpler font for the word 'Recruitment.' Playful loose fonts like this are often used for holiday agency companies.

We also created a colourful sun motif over the 'o.'

To do this, we used three capital 'I' letters, colouring, rotating, and resizing each of them individually. You could achieve the same effect with

a simple Quick Tear (convert the shape to curves—you'll find this command on the **Tools** menu—and then edit the shape as required.)

Example 3

This example builds on the previous themes and ideas. Here, the focus is on the sunrise over the letter 'i'. This logo has a more 'technical' look and feel, more appropriate for an I.T. job agency for example.

A clean and simple font was used, with the shade of each letter deepening towards the centre of the word. With this design, the letter 'i' and its sunrise motif could be used as a separate branding identity for the company.

Example 4

This example takes a very different direction. The heavy bold typeface (Arial Black) represents strength, while the colours were introduced to soften the company image. The letter spacing of the word 'RECRUITMENT' was expanded.

A simple, but effective technique—basic coloured Quick Shapes were used to add colour behind the letters.

While this logo has quite a generic look and feel, it would be very recognizable.

Example 5

Here, we've created a **typographic letterform** logo formed by placing the letters 'h' and 'r' one on top of the other. Again, we've used Quick Shapes for the coloured graphic bars.

Typographic letterform logos are preferred usually because of their effective means towards trademark development. This logo doesn't share the same themes as the previous examples (horizons, sunrises)—it's quite generic. It does, however, have strong distinctiveness, **retention**, **modularity**, and **equity**.

Modularity: Describes how well a logo can be used across multiple applications (different printed media for example). In particular, how a typographic letterform logo can be used in conjunction with its more traditional full title logo (in our example, 'Horizon Recruitment').

Retention: Used to describe the process of a viewer's first interaction with the logo. If a symbol is too easy to read and figure out, the viewer feels no sense of discovery—no personal investment or connection with the logo. Having to digest the logo and work it out (in this case from the letters h + r within the letterform) ensures the logo stays with them in the subconscious.

Equity: Refers to a logo's 'staying power' without the need to redesign. It is desirable to be modern and trendy—but not so much so that the logo may go out of fashion. It's generally better, therefore, to develop a more timeless identity.

Now that you have created your logo, why don't you add it to the **My Designs** category in the **Gallery** tab? To do this, **Ctrl**-drag a copy of the logo onto the tab. This will ensure that it is available to use throughout your PagePlus publications, just like any other gallery object.

If you need more logo ideas, don't forget that the **Gallery** tab has 100 different professional logos, and even more variations thereof, for you to customize for your own use.

For more information, see online Help and the **How To** tab.

In this example we have clearly conveyed a fast-moving, modern, and powerful corporate image. But this is just the beginning. A well-designed logo can be used for many different purposes—business stationery, brochures, newsletters, and so on.

We hope we've given you an insight into logo design, and inspired you to create a logo that will work for your company to promote a distinct and recognizable identity.

Designing a Nameplate

Great newsletters start with an effective nameplate. Learn how to create your own by adapting one of our pre-built designs.

We'll show you how to:

- Adapt a **LogoStudio** design to create a nameplate.
- Use a variety of typefaces to create different effects.
- Add your design to the gallery.

Designing a Nameplate

Among other things, nearly all newsletters will contain a **nameplate**, body text and headlines.

The **nameplate** provides a visual identity for the newsletter. It's usually found as a banner across the top (or down the side) of the front page. The nameplate contains the name of the newsletter, but it may also have graphics or a logo, and perhaps a subtitle, motto, and the publication information (Volume, Issue or Date).

We're going to add a customized nameplate to a **themed layout**.

To open a themed layout

1   On the **File** menu, click **New from Startup Wizard**.

    In the Startup Wizard, click the **Use Design Template** option.

2   In the dialog:

    • In the **Theme Layouts** list on the left, select the **Tickle** category.

    • In the centre pane, select the **Newsletter** template.

    • In the Scheme drop-down list, select **Scheme 2**.

    • Click **Open**.

3   In the **User Details** dialog click **Update**.

    The template opens as a new, one page document in the workspace. Now to add our nameplate. To get us started quickly, we're going to customize one of the logo designs in the **Gallery** tab.

Masthead or Nameplate?

Although it is sometimes used as an alternate name for a **nameplate**, the **masthead** is actually the section of a newsletter that lists the name of the publisher and other pertinent data. It may include staff names, contributors, subscription information, addresses, logo, etc.

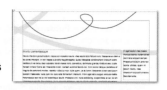

To create a nameplate

1 Click on the title frame to select it and press **Delete**.

2 On the **Gallery** tab, select the **Logos** category from the drop-down menu.

3 Scroll down to logo **34**. Then, click and drag it from the tab onto the page.

The **Insert Logo** dialog opens.

4 In the dialog:

- In the **Designs** pane, click the third design down.

- In the **Name** text box, type 'guitaramp'.

- In the **Motto** text box, type 'newsletter'.

- Click **OK**.

The nameplate is placed on the page.

5 Drag the ⊹ **Move** button to move the design into position within the margin guides and in the **Transform** tab:

- Click **Anchor Top Left**.

- Make sure **Aspect Ratio** is locked 🔒 (if unlocked the tab displays 🔓) and then change the height to **3.5 cm**.

The basic nameplate is in place, however, we can make it more eye-catching by editing it in **LogoStudio**. Let's do this now.

💡 You can use the **Fonts** tab to find, preview and apply any font. Many fonts have both a 'heavy' and a 'light' style. These can be used to add interest to title text without looking over-complicated or fussy.

For the next steps, we used the '**Seabird SF**' group of fonts that can be installed from the PagePlus Resource DVD.

To edit a logo in Logo Studio

1 With the logo selected, click the
   🖉 **Edit in LogoStudio** button.
   The logo opens for editing in
   LogoStudio.

2 Click and drag to select the word
   'guitar,' then, in the **Fonts** tab, click
   on a heavy version of your chosen
   font to apply it.

3 Click and drag to select the word
   'amp,' then, in the **Fonts** tab, click
   on a light version of your chosen font
   to apply it.

4 Next, click to select the 'newsletter'
   frame border - the frame turns grey to show it's selected.

5 In the **Fonts** tab, click to apply the same heavy font as before.

6 On the **Transform** tab, ensure
   Lock Aspect Ratio is off and then,
   change the height to **0.5 cm** and the
   width to **4.5 cm**.

7 Drag the ⊕ **Move**
   button to place the frame
   below the word 'guitar.'

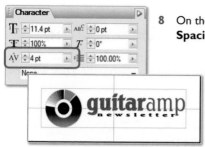

8   On the **Character** tab, change the
    Spacing to 4 pt.

The 'newsletter' text expands
to fit between the descenders
of 'g' and 'p'.

9   On the Tools toolbar, click the **A Artistic Text Tool** and click
    once on the page to create an insertion point. Type 'Winter 2009'.

10 Select the border of the new object
    and on the Text context toolbar,
    set the size to 9 pt.

11 On the Arrange toolbar, click
    Rotate Left. The text object
    rotates by 90°.

12 Finally, drag the
    object into
    position and
    resize so that it
    is the same
    height as the
    letter 'p.'

13 Click **Close LogoStudio** to return to the
    main PagePlus workspace.

    Your nameplate is complete! By making
    these simple adjustments to font style, size,
    and spacing, we have created contrast—
    an important element in any type of
    publication layout.

    Now that we've spent time creating
    our nameplate, we can save a copy of
    it in the **Gallery** tab to make it
    available for every new publication.

To add an object to the gallery

1   On the **Gallery** tab, in the category drop-down list, select **My Designs**.

2   On the page, click to select the nameplate object—the frame will turn grey to show it is selected.

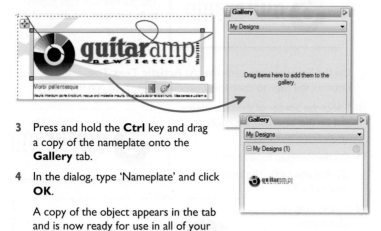

3   Press and hold the **Ctrl** key and drag a copy of the nameplate onto the **Gallery** tab.

4   In the dialog, type 'Nameplate' and click **OK**.

A copy of the object appears in the tab and is now ready for use in all of your future projects!

> 💡 When you first drag an object into an empty gallery category, PagePlus automatically creates a sub-category in which to store your objects. As you use the gallery more and more, you may choose to add your own sub-categories to organize your designs. For information, see *Using the Gallery* in online Help.

Projects

Aimed at both beginners and more experienced PagePlus users, these illustrated projects provide you with the opportunity to experiment with various tools and techniques.

In each project, you'll create a different type of document, picking up valuable tips and tricks along the way.

Real Estate Flyer

PagePlus provides a wide selection of design templates, which you can use as starting points for your own publications.

In this project, we'll start with a real estate flyer template and customize it to suit our own requirements. You can use the same principles to customize any of the design templates.

In this exercise, you'll learn how to:

- Work with master pages.
- Update user details.
- Move and align objects.
- Replace, add, resize, and crop images.
- Insert logos.
- Apply colour fills.
- Add pages.
- Preview and print a double-sided publication.

Real Estate Flyer

This project assumes that you'll be printing your flyer on A4 or Letter sized paper, and that you are using the sample images provided in the **...\Workspace\Real Estate** folder. In a standard installation, you'll find this folder in the following location:

C:\Program Files\Serif\PagePlus\X4\Tutorials

If you prefer, you can use your own images.

I. Updating the template

The first section of this tutorial shows you how to edit and update the existing elements of the template publication.

To open the design template

1   On the **File** menu, click **New from Startup Wizard**.

2   In the Startup Wizard, click **Use Design Template**.

3   In the **Choose a Template** dialog, in the left **Templates** pane, expand the **Flyers & Posters > Flyers** subcategory.

> If you've switched the Startup Wizard off, you can switch it back on.
>
> I   Click **Tools > Options**.
>
> 2   In the **Options** dialog, on the **General** page, click to select the **Use startup wizard** check box.

4   Click **A4 > Portrait** or **Letter > Portrait** (depending on your product version) and view the thumbnail samples on the right.

5   Select the **Real Estate Listing** template and click **OK**.

6   If the **User Details** dialog opens, click **Cancel** to close it (we'll return to this dialog later).

This is a single page publication containing a selection of images, text objects, and shapes.

Let's start by replacing the images of the property with our own.

To replace an image

1 Click on the main image and then click the  **Replace Picture** button.

2 In the **Import Picture** dialog, browse to your ...**Workspace\Real Estate** folder.

3 Select the **6294764.jpg** file and click **Open**.

4 The photo is updated on the page and automatically scaled to fit.

5 Repeat the previous steps to replace the other photos of the house with **5321355.jpg** and **6294768.jpg**, as illustrated on the right.

Our next task is to replace the photo of the realtor.

As this image has been placed on the **master page**, we need to be in Master Page view to work with this object.

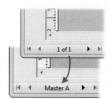

To view and update the master page

1 In the lower left corner of the workspace, click the **Current Page** box (currently showing that you are viewing page '1 of 1') to switch to Master Page view.

> 🔖 Typically, a master page is used for storing elements that appear on multiple pages of a publication—a logo, background, page numbers, and so on.

In this publication, the photo of the realtor, the company information, and the decorative background elements have been placed on the master page.

2 Select the photo. Because this image has been placed inside a picture frame, additional controls display beneath it.

3 Click ▶ **Replace Picture** and replace the photo with **1513h0004.jpg**.

4 Click 🖐 **Pan** and drag on the image to reposition it inside its frame.

Picture frames are shaped containers similar to text frames. You can use these as placeholders, and then import or drag your pictures into them. At any time you can swap a different picture into the same frame. This allows you to separate the container from its content, and incorporate picture frames into your layout irrespective of the actual images that will go inside them.

For details, see *Adding picture frames* in online Help.

Now let's update the company information. This is taken directly from user details fields, which means that we can make all our edits in the **User Details** dialog and then update everything at once.

To update user details

1 On the **Tools** menu, click **Set User Details**.

2 In the **User Details** dialog, on the **Business** tab, click and drag to highlight the default text and then type in your own information.

3 When you've finished, click **Update**.

On the page, the text is updated automatically.

You can create your own custom user details fields on the **Custom** tab of the **User Details** dialog.

---

4   (Optional) To insert additional user details fields, click **Insert > Information > User Details**, select the field to add and click **OK**.

As the length of your user details will probably differ from the original fields, you may need to reposition or realign some of your text objects.

To move a text object

- Select the object and then click and drag the  **Move** button that displays in the upper left corner.

  - or -

- Click to select the text object's border (the border changes colour to show that the entire object is selected), and then drag into position using the **Move** cursor.

To align objects

1   Use the **Pointer Tool** to select the objects you want to align. To do this, you can:

   - Click and drag to draw a bounding box around the objects.

     - or -

   - Hold down the **Shift** key and click each object in turn.

2   On the **Align** tab, click your required alignment option(s).

While we're on the master page, let's also replace the logo. We'll show you two ways to do this:

- By inserting a predesigned logo (which you can edit in **LogoStudio**). You might choose this method if you don't already have a company logo and want some ideas, or a starting point, for creating one.

- By inserting your own logo graphic file. Use this method if you already have a company logo and want to add it to your flyer.

To insert a LogoStudio logo

1 Select the logo graphic and then press the **Delete** key.

2 On the Tools toolbar, click
    Insert Logo.

3 In the **Insert Logo** dialog,
    browse the thumbnails and
    select the logo of your
    choice.

4 To apply the colour
    scheme of your publication
    to the logo, clear the
    Apply colour set check
    box.

    - or -

    To apply a colour set independent of the
    publication colour scheme, select the **Apply
    colour set** check box and choose a colour set
    from the drop-down list.

5 Click **Open**.

    To insert the logo at default size, simply click the
    mouse; to set the logo size, click and drag.

💡 You can also place your logo by dragging it
from the **Logos** category in the **Gallery** tab
directly onto the page.

To edit the logo, click 📝 **Edit in LogoStudio**
to open the LogoStudio window.

To insert your own logo

1 Select the logo graphic and press the **Delete** key.

2 On the Tools toolbar, click 🖼 **Import Picture**.

3 In the **Import Picture** dialog, browse to and select your own logo graphic file and then click **Open**.

4 Click and drag on your page to set the size of the logo, then drag into position on your page.

Before returning to Normal page view, let's change the colour of the background elements.

To apply a colour fill

1 Click to select the large blue rectangle.

2 On the **Swatches** tab, click the ⬜ **Fill** button (currently showing that this object has a blue fill applied).

3 Click to expand the ▦▾ **Palettes** drop down list and select the palette of your choice.

4 Click a colour swatch to apply the colour fill to the selected shape.

5 Repeat the previous steps to apply colour fills to the other two shapes.

6 Click the **Current Page** box to return to Normal page view.

In Normal page view, we can see another colour fill we need to adjust.

7 Follow the previous steps to apply a complementary colour fill to the central horizontal band.

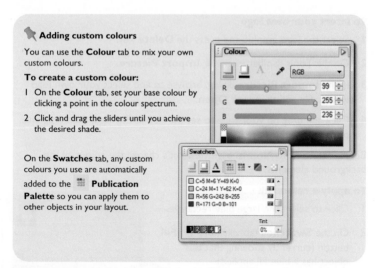

Adding custom colours

You can use the **Colour** tab to mix your own custom colours.

To create a custom colour:

1 On the **Colour** tab, set your base colour by clicking a point in the colour spectrum.

2 Click and drag the sliders until you achieve the desired shade.

On the **Swatches** tab, any custom colours you use are automatically added to the **Publication Palette** so you can apply them to other objects in your layout.

Let's now turn our attention to the text objects. We need to update these with the details of our listing.

In PagePlus, you can use the **Pointer Tool** to select, edit, and format text directly on the page,

To select and edit text

1 Click the **Pointer Tool** and then:

- Drag to select a range of text.

  - or -

- Double-click to select a word.

  - or -

- Triple-click to select a paragraph.

  The selected text area is shaded in blue for clear editing.

2 Type in your own text as required.

To apply formatting and colour to text

Select the text and then:

- To apply character and paragraph formatting, use the controls on the Text context toolbar.

- To apply colour, click  **A Text** on the **Swatches** tab, and then click a colour swatch.

💡 For quick and easy formatting and recolouring of an entire text object:

1 Select the text object by clicking on its border (the border changes colour).

2 Use the Text context toolbar and/or **Swatches** tab as described above.

When you have finished making your changes, you're ready to preview and print your flyer.

To preview a publication

1 On the Standard toolbar, click 🔾 **Print Preview** to see how your flyer will appear on the printed page.

2 If you are happy with the results, click 🖨 **Print**.

3 In the **Print** dialog, set your printer options and the number of copies to print, and then click **Print**.

2. Adding new content

We've updated the template objects with our own information, and these changes may well be sufficient for your needs. But now let's suppose you want to create a double-sided flyer and add more text and images.

The final section of this tutorial shows how to:

- Add new master and standard pages.

- Import, resize, and crop images.

- Create artistic and frame text.

- Print double-sided documents.

Adding pages

We'll create a new master page and assign it to a new publication page.

To create a new master page

1   At the top of the **Pages** tab, click to expand the upper **Master Pages** panel, currently displaying just the one page— **Master A**.

2   Click the 🖻 **Page Manager** button.

3   In the **Master Page Manager** dialog, click the **Add** tab.

4   Select the **Copy layers from** and **Copy objects** check boxes. Click **OK**.

5   The new master page—**Master B**—is created and opened in the workspace.

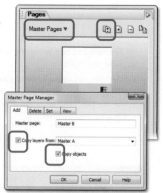

This page is an identical copy of Master A. We want to keep all the same page objects, except for the realtor photo and details.

6   Using the ⬉ **Pointer Tool**, click and drag to draw a bounding box around the photograph and its text frame.

7   Press the **Delete** key to remove these objects from the page.

Jane Jones
jjones@jjones&corealty.com
www.jjones&corealty.com

Our next task is to assign the new master page to a new publication page.

To create a new standard page

1 On the **Pages** tab, in the lower **Pages** panel, click the  **Page Manager** button.

2 In the **Page Manager** dialog, click the **Insert** tab.

3 In the **Master page** drop-down list, select **Master B**. Click **OK**.

The new page is added to the publication and opened in the workspace.

Working with images

You can add images by importing them directly onto the page, or you can use the **Media Bar** to temporarily store your images before placing them.

To import an image

1 On the Tools toolbar, click  **Import Picture**.

2 In the **Import Picture** dialog, browse to and select an image (to select multiple images, hold down the **Ctrl** key and then click each image in turn).

3 Click **Open**.

4 Click on your page to place each image at the default size, or click and drag to set the size of each image.

To add images to the Media Bar

1 At the bottom of the workspace, click the ▬▲▬ handle to display the **Media Bar**.

2 On the **Media Bar**, in the rightmost drop-down list, select **Temporary Album**.

3 Click 🎇 **Add Image**.

4   In the **Open** dialog, browse to the ...**Workspace\\Real Estate**
    folder.

5   Press and hold down the **Ctrl** key and select the **6294750.jpg** and
    6294792.jpg files. Click **Open**.

    The images display as thumbnails in
    the **Media Bar**.

> 💡 You can also drag an image file from any
> Windows folder directly onto the **Media Bar**.

6   To place an image, drag its thumbnail
    from the **Media Bar** onto the page.

    Images that have been added to the
    publication are marked with a green
    checkmark.

By default, images are added to a
temporary album, but you can create
more permanent albums from which you
can retrieve stored images at any time.

To create a named album

1   Click 🌐 New Album .

2   In the **New Album** dialog, type a name for the album, and then click
    🖼 **Add Image** or 🗂 **Add Folder**.

3   In the dialog, navigate to and select an image file, or the folder
    containing your images.

4   Click **Open** to add the
    list of images to the
    dialog.

5   (Optional) In the
    Placement drop-down
    list, choose whether to
    link or embed images.

6   Click **OK**.

Once placed on the page, you may need to resize or crop your imported images.

To resize an image

1 Select the image.

2 Click one of the corner selection handles and drag to a new position.

To crop an image

1 Select the image.

2 On the Attributes toolbar, on the Crop flyout, click the ⊓ **Square Crop Tool**.

3 Click and drag an edge or corner handle towards the centre of the image.

4 (Optional) To apply a feathered edge to the crop outline, use the **Feather** drop-down menu on the Crop context toolbar.

Adding text

PagePlus lets you create both **artistic text** and standard and shaped **text frames**.

- **Artistic text** is generally used for standalone text with special effects. When you resize an artistic text object, the text resizes accordingly.

- **Text frames** work equally well for single words, standalone paragraphs, or multi page articles. Text inside a text frame remains the same size when you resize the frame.

To create artistic text

1 On the Text flyout, click the A **Artistic Text Tool**.

2 To create text at the default size, click on the page and start typing.

- or -

To set the size of the text, click and drag with the cross-hair cursor to set the desired text size, and then start typing.

> **Setting text properties**
>
> - To set artistic or frame text properties before typing: Use the controls on the Text context toolbar.
> - To set text colour before typing: On the **Swatches** or **Colour** tab, click the **A** **Text** button, and then click a colour.

To create a text frame

1 On the Tools toolbar, on the Text Frames flyout, click the **Standard Text Frame** (for a standard rectangular frame), or choose one of the **Shaped Frame** tools.

2 To create a new frame at a default size, click on the page.

- or -

To set the size of the frame, click and drag.

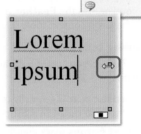

3 To add text, simply start typing.

4 If required, click and drag to adjust the dimensions of the frame.

When you're happy with page 2 of your flyer, you're ready to print.

Printing double-sided documents

If your printer supports duplex (two-sided) printing, you can automatically print out your publication as a double-sided document by setting the double-sided printing options in the PagePlus **Print** dialog.

If your printer does not support duplex printing, you can use the **Manual Duplex Printing Wizard** to configure your standard printer to print on both sides of your paper.

To print on a printer that supports duplex printing

1   On the Standard toolbar, click 🖶 **Print**.

2   In the **Print** dialog, on the **General** tab, choose your printer and then select an option from the **Double-sided options** drop-down list:

   • To print on both sides, flipping on the short side of the paper, select **Automatic Duplex, flip short side**.

   • To print on both sides, flipping on the long side of the paper, select **Automatic Duplex**.

3   Click **Print**.

To print using manual duplex printing

1   On the Standard toolbar, click 🖶 **Print**.

2   In the **Print** dialog, on the **General** tab, select the printer that you want to use and then select **Manual Duplex** from the **Double-sided options** drop-down list.

> 🔖 Double-sided printing is only available for publications that have at least two pages.

3   On the **Duplex** tab, select your preferred options from the drop-down lists.

4   To set up your printer:

   • Click **Set up Manual Duplex**.

   • Follow the Wizard instructions, selecting the options that apply to your printout and following instructions where prompted.

     The options you choose should mirror those you set in the drop-down lists on the **Duplex** tab.

   • Click **Next** to proceed through the setup. Click **Finish**.

5   On the **General** tab, set your print range and number of copies to print.

6   Click **Print**.

7 The first page will print. Place the paper back in the tray and press continue to print the other side.

You should now have a double-sided printout!

In this tutorial, we've introduced you to the basic tools and techniques required to create and customize the key components of a PagePlus document—pages, text, and images.

Of course, PagePlus provides numerous other features, but the topics we've covered here should be sufficient for many of your desktop publishing projects.

Business Card

PagePlus tools give you the flexibility to lay out text and graphic objects, and design logos for your business cards—and it's easy to set up your printer to print multiple copies on one sheet. Creating your own design also allows you to make modifications on the fly, and then preview and print out your results before choosing a final layout. We'll show you how to:

- Set up page and printer options.
- Lay out a small publication.

You can use any logo to complete this tutorial, either one you've already completed, a sample logo or you could use one of the designs in the **Logo** category of **Gallery** tab. For more help, see the **Adding content > Adding logos** section in the **How To** tab.

Business Card

You may have noticed that some business cards look better than others. Why is this? Is it the layout, the colours, the typeface, or a combination of all of these elements? Great designs are not a mystery and you don't need professional graphic design skills to produce a business card. By following some simple rules, you can ensure that your business cards look professional and convey the right image.

To set up a business card publication

1 Open PagePlus, click **File**, point to **New**, click **New from Startup Wizard**, and then click **Start New Publication**.

2 In the dialog, click **Small Publications**, and then click **Business Cards**. Click the **Wide Business Card** template, and then click **OK**.

3 On the **File** menu, click **Page Setup**, then click **Create Custom** to open the **Small Publication Setup** dialog.

  • The left preview pane shows how the business cards will be laid out at print time.

  • In the **Size** section, the default **Width** (8.50 cm) and **Height** (5.50 cm) of a 'wide business card' document are displayed.

  • The **Gap X** and **Gap Y** values denote the size of the spaces that will be left between the business cards when they are laid out side-by-side on one sheet of paper.

  • In the **Margins** section, clear the **Auto** box to set your own page margin size, or leave it selected to use the PagePlus default settings.

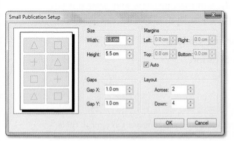

  • The **Layout** section tells you how many business cards will fit across and down a single page, using the current margin and gap settings.

> If you've bought special business card paper, you'll find all of these dimensions on the template that is usually supplied with the pack.

Let's remove the gap between the business cards so that we won't have to cut out each card individually after we have printed them.

4   Set both the **Gap X** and **Gap Y** values to '0.' In the preview pane, you'll notice that the layout changes to reflect the new settings. Note also that we can now fit ten cards to a page, rather than eight.

5   Click **OK** to return to the **Page Setup** dialog. Click the **Print Setup** button.

6   In the **Print Setup** dialog, click the **Properties** button.

The dialog that opens is printer-specific—the settings depend on the printer you're using.

The **Orientation** setting is generally available regardless of the printer and lets you choose whether to print your page in **Portrait** or **Landscape** style.

When printing small publications such as business cards, try changing the orientation and then checking back in the **Page Setup** dialog to see which orientation will fit more copies on a single page.

7   Click **OK** three times to close the printer, **Print Setup**, and **Page Setup** dialogs.

We've set up our business card publication. We're going to work on our logo design next, so we don't need the business card document at the moment. Let's save it and keep it open as we'll need to come back to it later.

• On the **File** menu, click **Save**. Save the document as **Business Card.ppp**.

• Follow the steps outlined previously to create a new blank document. This time select a **Regular/Normal** 'Portrait' size document.

You'll use this new document to experiment with your logo design. Once you've settled on a final layout, you can then copy it on to your business card.

A **logo** is a unique name, symbol, or trademark of a company or organization. Well-designed logos provide brand name recognition and promote a business presence. They achieve this because people process an image in their mind more easily than words. In addition, visual stimulation produces a more effective and long-lasting impact on the audience's memory than words alone.

Business Card

A business card should be laid out in a way that is balanced. Different areas saying different things and presenting different information, all in order of appropriateness.

Take a look at our example for a fictitious company called 'Horizon Recruitment.' It's appropriate that the company logo is the focal point. The aim of this business card is to promote the company, while providing a means of direct contact with the person who gives away the card. (You can find this logo example in the tutorial, *Designing a Logo*.)

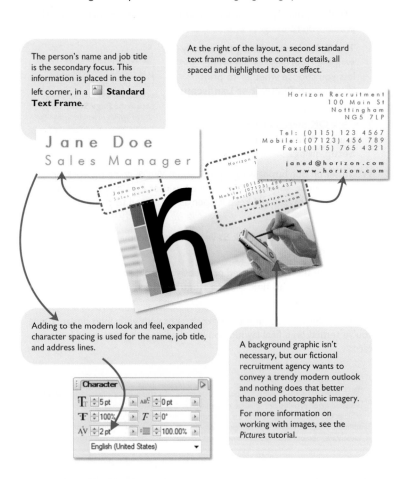

The person's name and job title is the secondary focus. This information is placed in the top left corner, in a 🖼 **Standard Text Frame**.

At the right of the layout, a second standard text frame contains the contact details, all spaced and highlighted to best effect.

Adding to the modern look and feel, expanded character spacing is used for the name, job title, and address lines.

A background graphic isn't necessary, but our fictional recruitment agency wants to convey a trendy modern outlook and nothing does that better than good photographic imagery.

For more information on working with images, see the *Pictures* tutorial.

To lay out a business card

1 Open the publication in which you created your logo. (We used the logo created in the *Designing a Logo* tutorial.)

2 Select your entire logo design and then on the **Edit** menu, click **Copy** (or press **Ctrl+C**).

3 Now return to your business card document by clicking on its document tab.

4 On the **Edit** menu, click **Paste** (or press **Ctrl+V**) to paste your logo into the document.

5 With the logo selected, resize it by clicking one of the frame handles, holding down the left mouse button, and then dragging to the new size.

6 Drag the resized logo into position on the business card.

7 On the Tools toolbar, click the 🔲 **Standard Text Frame** tool, then click and drag to insert a frame in the top left corner.

> 🔖 When you paste or import a new image, or select an existing one, note that the **Picture** tools display in the context toolbar.

8 In the text frame, type your name, press **Enter**, and then type your job title.

9 In the text frame, click and drag to select the text (or press **Ctrl+A**).

10 On the Text context toolbar, choose the font size and style for your heading, adjust the letter spacing if necessary.

11 Add a second text frame to the right of the logo.

Type in the company name and address, and your contact details.

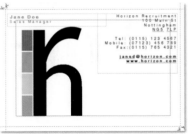

Although a background graphic isn't necessary (and may sometimes be inappropriate), in our example, it certainly adds visual appeal and interest.

It's easy to do this:

- Simply click  **Import Picture**, and choose your image.

- Once you have the image in place, select it, and then on the toolbar, click the **Send to Back** button to place it behind all the other objects on the page.

💡 You can also add a background graphic to a master page. For more information on master pages, see the *Master Pages* tutorial, or refer to the PagePlus online Help.

We hope we've given you an insight into business card design and inspired you to create business cards that will work for your company to promote a distinct and recognizable identity. For more information on logo design, see the *Designing a Logo* tutorial.

Greetings Card

happy birthday

Whether it's to celebrate a birthday, an anniversary, or a graduation, or simply to tell a friend you are thinking of them, we all enjoy sending and receiving greetings cards. With PagePlus, you can impress family and friends and make that special event even more memorable by making your own greetings card from scratch.

In this project, you'll learn how to:

- Lay out a folded publication.
- Work with a variety of images to create very different effects.
- Create and format text.
- Adjust image colour.
- Use the **Styles** tab to add a variety of effects.
- Add a **Gallery** flash.
- Select the right paper for your greetings card.
- Print a greetings card.

Greetings Card

In this project, we'll create four different greetings card designs, which you can print on a home printer. We've supplied sample images for you to use; you'll find them in the **...\Workspace\Greeting Card** folder of your PagePlus installation directory

(usually **C:\Program Files\Serif\PagePlus\X4\Tutorials**).

We'll start by creating and saving a blank document.

To create and save a greetings card document

1   In PagePlus, click **File**, point to **New**, click **New from Startup Wizard**, and then click **Start New Publication**.

2   In the dialog, click **Folded**, and then click **Greetings Cards**. Click the first template—**Card**—and then click **Open**.

3   To save the new document, click **File**, then **Save**.

Now to import the image for our greetings card.

To import and position an image

1   On the Tools toolbar, click
    📷 ▾ **Import Picture**.

2   In the **Import Picture** dialog, browse to the
    ...\Workspace\Greeting Card folder and open the **Flower.jpg** file.

3   When the cursor changes to ⁺📷 click on the page to insert the image. (Note that the Picture tools are displayed in the context toolbar.)

> 💡 Before importing into PagePlus, an image of a detailed flower was opened in PhotoPlus. The background was then removed to produce a clean and contemporary design.
>
> The same effect can also be produced using PagePlus' Image Cutout Studio. For more information, see online Help or the **How To** tab.

4   Resize the image by clicking one of its corner handles and dragging it to a new position. Make this image about 6 cm by 6 cm.

Let's add the title. We want it to match the look and feel of the image, so we'll use a modern font style.

Use the **Fonts** tab to view your currently installed fonts and apply them to your text objects.

Select your text, then hover over a listed font for an in-place preview—simply click to apply the font to your text.

The tab also hosts a **quick search** feature to filter fonts by name, attribute, or type.

To create a title using artistic text

1   On the Tools toolbar, click the
    A Artistic Text tool, click about 2 cm below the image and type 'happy birthday'.

2   Click in the text and press **Ctrl+A** to select both words. On the Text context toolbar, choose the font style for your heading. We used Arial 18 pt.

3   With the text frame selected, click the **Character** tab at the lower right of the workspace.

4   Expand the character spacing to 10.0 pt.

    To do this either, click the 'up' arrow, or click the 'right' arrow and then drag the slider.

Let's position our image and title so that they are centred horizontally on the page. PagePlus offers us a precise method of aligning objects on a page using the **Align** tab.

To align objects on a page

1   Press and hold down the **Shift** key, then use the **▶ Pointer Tool** to click on the image and the text object. A blue bounding box appears around both objects.

2   On the **Align** tab:

    • In the **Relative to:** drop-down list, select **Page**.

    • Click **♈ Centre Horizontally.**

For a quick and easy effect, we'll bold and change the colour of the first letters of the title words; we'll then add a subtle reflection.

To change font colour

1 In the text frame, click and drag to select the letter 'h.'

2 On the **Swatches** tab, select the **Standard RGB** palette from the ▦ ⁃ **Palette** flyout.

3 Click the ⬛ **Text** button and choose one of the pink swatches—we used RGB (255, 127, 255).

4 With the letter still selected, click the **B Bold** button on the Text context toolbar.

We can now copy and paste the formatting of the letter 'h'.

h a p p y   b i r t h d a y

5 Press **Ctrl+C** to copy the selected letter 'h' and then, select the letter 'b' and click **Edit > Paste Format**.

Now to add a reflection. This effect looks impressive, but with the **Styles** tab, it's achieved with a click of a button! We're applying the reflection to an artistic text object but it works equally well on shapes, images, and other objects.

To add a reflection effect to an object

1 Select the text object.

2 On the **Styles** tab, in the category drop-down list, select the **Reflection** category.

3 In the **Artistic Text Reflections** sub-category, click on **Text Reflection 03** swatch.

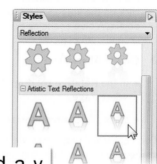

The reflection is applied. However, because our text has descenders, the 'tails' on the letters p and y, the reflection needs to be tweaked slightly.

happy birthday

4 On the Attributes toolbar, click the *fx* **Filter Effects** button.

5 In the **Filter Effects** dialog, drag the **Offset** slider to the right to increase the distance between the text and the reflection. The effect immediately updates, both in the dialog preview window (if open), and on the page.

6 When you are happy with the effect, click **OK**.

h a p p y   b i r t h d a y

You've created the layout for your first greetings card! As you can see, it doesn't require complicated procedures, or professional graphic design skills. In fact, the simplest designs often work the best.

To further demonstrate this point, we'll show you a few more examples, all of which use simple techniques that you can adapt to suit your own needs.

happy birthday

💡 Try to avoid importing very large image files. Even if these are scaled down on the publication page, the original file size is preserved. As a rule, downscale your images first using photo-editing software (such as PhotoPlus), then import them into PagePlus.

For this party invitation, the main photo was taken at an interesting angle, giving the composition some depth.

Again, a minimal palette of colours was used, the colours of the image being reproduced in the title. We used the same technique described above to create the reflection effect.

PARTY

happy birthday

For this textured abstract design, we started with an image of a vibrant textile. We cropped the photograph to show the detail of the fabric texture (you could do this with photo-editing software, or in PagePlus itself), and then placed it in the centre of the composition.

The colours of the text were then matched to the textile. To do this, we used the ✏ **Colour Picker** on the **Colour** tab.

For details, see the *Colour Schemes* tutorial.

The next few examples show how you can turn an everyday photo of a pet or family member into a fun greetings card.

We imported our photo and then altered its colour properties by using the **Swatches** tab and the image adjustment buttons on the Picture context toolbar.

To quickly recolour an image

1 With the image selected, click the ▤ **Fill** button on the **Swatches** tab. Choose a colour from the palette— generally darker colours work best for this technique (for example, brown will create a sepia effect).

2 Use the brightness (◔ increase and ◑ decrease) and contrast (◑ increase and ◔ decrease) buttons from the Picture context toolbar to adjust image levels.

To give the piece a more finished feel, we also added a line border to the image.

To add a line border to an image

1 Click to select the image.

2 To add the line, on the **Line** tab:

- Select a line style from the drop-down menu (we selected a double line style).

- Drag the slider to the right to increase the line weight.

- Click to select a **Stroke Alignment** style (we chose **Align Outer**).

3 To change the line colour, on the **Swatch** tab, click the ⬜ **Line** button and click a colour swatch.

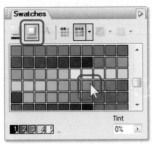

For the finishing touch we added a caption. A big, bold, fun font is used to good effect here. For consistency, we used the same colour for the text as we chose for the line border.

In this example, we imported our photo and then applied a fun-shaped crop using a QuickShape.

To crop to a shape

1 Import an image.

2 On the Tools toolbar, select a QuickShape from the **QuickShape** flyout. (We selected a **Quick Star**.)

3   Drag on the page to draw the QuickShape and use the nodes to change the shape as necessary.

4   Position the shape over the area to crop.

5   Select the QuickShape and the picture beneath it and on the **Tools** menu, click **Crop to Shape.**

> The image is revealed.

> 💡 You can position the image within the crop using the ▢ **Square Crop Tool**. For more information see the **How To** tab or online Help.

In our final example, we imported our image and added a filter effect from the **Styles** tab.

To add a filter effect

1   Click to select the image.

2   On the **Styles** tab, in the category drop-down list, select the **Bevels** category.

3   In the **3D** sub-category, click on **Small Bottom Right** swatch.

> The effect is applied and immediately, the image is lifted from the page.

Thank you!

The inside pages

When you are happy with the front of your card layout, you're ready to add greetings to the inside pages—even a verse if you're feeling really creative! However, to take out the hard work, why not add one of the flashes from the **Gallery** tab.

To add a flash from the Gallery tab

1 On the **Gallery** tab, in the category drop-down list, click **Flashes**.

All of the designs available for selection are displayed in the main section of the tab.

2 Drag the design you want to use onto your page.

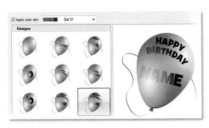

3 A dialog opens, displaying variations of the selected design.

Click to select the variation you want to use.

4 At the top of the dialog, the **Apply colour set** check box is selected by default. The adjacent drop-down list provides colour sets specifically designed to complement the design.

Select the colour set you prefer.

- or -

To apply the colour scheme currently used in your document, clear the **Apply colour set** check box.

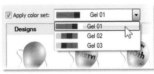

5 If your flash contains a name and/or message you can edit the text by typing directly into the text box(es).

6 To add the design to your page, click **OK**.

The design is inserted at default size.

If required, you can resize it by clicking and dragging a corner resize handle.

Tips for printing

You can buy packs of pre-folded greetings card paper and envelopes from most office suppliers. Usually, this paper is specifically intended to be used with inkjet home printers, and comes in 160 gsm weight.

When you select or define a **Folded Publication** (as we did at the beginning of this exercise), PagePlus automatically performs imposition of folded publications. The settings ensure that two or four pages of the publication are printed on each sheet of paper. This saves you from having to calculate how to position and collate pairs of pages on a single larger page.

That's all there is to it! We've shown you several examples of greetings cards to start you off, and hopefully inspire you to create your own unique designs. As you can see, all it takes is a little time and imagination.

To produce professional-looking, double-sided sheets, why not take advantage of PagePlus's duplex printing feature? It enables you to achieve great double-sided printing results, even if you don't have a printer capable of automatic duplex printing. See the section *Manual Duplex Printing* in online Help for more information.

It's worth experimenting with printing your cards on everyday paper first, to get everything (margins, positioning etc.) set up correctly.

PDF Web Form

In this project, you'll create a PDF form that can be used to collect user data online.

In this exercise, you'll learn how to:

- Design a layout for a functional form.
- Add form fields and set properties.
- Publish a PDF form.

PDF Web Form

To introduce you to the world of PDF forms, we're going to create a simple form to allow users to sign up to a newsletter. Along the way, we'll show you some of the valuable tools available in PagePlus.

However, before we dive in and start placing form objects, there are a couple of things to do first that will save us time in the long run. Use a blank piece of paper to complete these initial steps.

Creating the form design

Let's think about the information we need to collect from our potential newsletter recipients. At the very least, we'll need to know who is subscribing and their email address. However, we could also get some information that might be useful for marketing campaigns at a later date.

Let's assume that we want to capture the following data:

- Name (first and last)
- Email address
- Age
- Gender
- Whether or not they want to be informed of other offers

💡 Design guidelines

- Keep your form simple and uncluttered.
- Group related form fields together.
- Give your form fields clear, meaningful labels and position them consistently relative to the object.
- Provide clear and simple instructions (use ToolTips where necessary) to help users complete the form as easily as possible.
- If users must complete certain information on the form, be sure to indicate that these fields are mandatory. For example, with an asterisk or colour-coding.

The next step is to map out the form design with paper and pencil. Although it's tempting to skip this part, try not to. If you sketch your form layout on paper first, you'll end up with a better overall design and save time as you'll only place the objects that you really want.

To continue an earlier theme, we're going to use a design to match the poster that we created in the *Artistic Text* tutorial. You'll find a project file **form.ppp** in the **...\Workspace\Form** folder.

In a standard installation, this is found in:

C:\Program Files\Serif\PagePlus\X4\Tutorials

We drafted out the form design illustrated here.

All we need to do now is recreate it in PagePlus. Let's get started...

To open the workspace document

1   On the **File** menu, click **Open...**

2   In the dialog, browse to the **Workspace** folder, select **anaconda.ppp** and click **Open**.

    The document opens in the workspace.

3   Next, on the **File** menu, click **Save As...**

4   Name the document **PDF form.ppp** and click **Save**.

Layout aids

The document has been set up using a 5 x 5 layout grid. If you can't see the grid, on the **View** menu, ensure that **Trimmed Mode** is unselected and that **Guide Lines** are selected. This will help you to position the elements.

Now we're ready to start creating our form.

Creating the form text and labels

The form we've designed has two distinct object types: text objects (information and labels—blue) and form objects (for user data—red). We'll add the text objects first.

We'll assume that you're already familiar with using text objects so we'll summarize this section. If you need more help with any of the steps, see the *Artistic Text* and *Frame Text* tutorials, refer to the **How To** tab or see online Help.

To add the title and information text

1   On the Tools toolbar, click the  **Standard Text Frame** tool.

2   Click and drag on the page to place a text frame approximately 1cm high and 14.7 cm (4 columns) wide.

3   On the Text context toolbar, select the Title Col style and type in the title, 'NEW PRODUCTS FROM ANACONDA'.

4   Once again, click the  **Standard Text Frame** tool.

5   Click and drag on the page to place a text frame below the title frame.

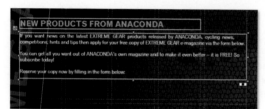

The text frame should be approximately 3.5 cm high and should span all 5 columns of the layout grid.

6   On the Text context toolbar, select the **Body Text Normal** style and type your introductory text. Alternatively, press **F5** to add placeholder text.

Next we'll place our form labels.

7   Click the  **Standard Text Frame** tool. Starting just below the previous frame, click and drag in the second column of the layout grid to place a text frame 1 column wide and approximately 0.7 cm high.

8   On the Text context toolbar, select the **Body Text Normal** style and click ≡ **Align Right**.

Dynamic Guides

To easily line up multiple objects, why not turn on **Dynamic Guides**?

- Click the arrow on the 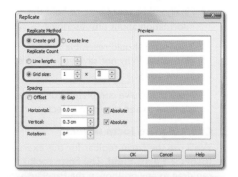 ▼ **Snapping** button. From the flyout menu, select **Dynamic Guides**.

For more information, see online Help.

From our form design, we know that we need 6 form items. Before we type our first label name, let's save ourselves some effort by using the **Replicate** dialog to make copies our newly created text box.

9 With the text box still selected, on the **Edit** menu, click **Replicate...**

10 In the dialog:

- Select **Replicate Method** to **Create grid**.

- Set the **Replicate Count** to **Grid size**, 1 × **6**.

- Set the **Spacing** to **Gap** and change the **Horizontal** spacing to **0.0** cm and the **Vertical** spacing to **0.3** cm.

- Click **OK**.

The six text frames appear neatly aligned on the page.

11 Click inside the first text box and type the label, 'First Name'.

12 In the subsequent text boxes, add the labels for:

- *Last Name
- *E-mail
- *Age
- *Gender
- Check this box to be informed of our special offers.

13 Resize the final text frame to fit the text by dragging the lower left corner handle of the frame to the left of the page.

14 Finally, add a text frame to hold the information about unsubscribing.

Your form should resemble the one illustrated. Why not save your progress at this point?

Now that we've completed our labels, it's time to add the form objects.

Creating the form objects

We'll use the Form toolbar for this exercise, but you can also click **Insert > Form Field**. The Form toolbar is a floating toolbar, which you can drag to any position in the PagePlus workspace.

To view the Form toolbar

- On the **View** menu, click Toolbars and then click **Form**.

The buttons on the toolbar represent the form field types available. For our first three fields we want users to type in their names and email address. For each of these we'll use a **text field**.

To create a text field

1 On the Form toolbar, click the 🔲 **Text Field** button.

2 Move the cursor next to the 'First Name' label and click and drag to insert the field.
Make sure that the field spans two columns of the layout grid.

Text field properties

Each text field can have its properties customized. To do this, right-click the field and then click **Form Field Properties**.

Within the dialog, you can adjust settings such as:

- Give a unique name to the field.
- Add a ToolTip to give the user information about the data field.
- Format the line around the text box, and the text that the user types into the box.
- Limit the number of letters that can be typed into the box.

For more information see online Help or the screen tutorial, *Creating a PDF Expenses Form*.

3 Right-click the text field and then click **Form Field Properties**.

4 In the **Name** text box, type 'First_Name'. Click **OK**.

5 Repeat steps 1 and 4 to add two more text fields next to the 'Last Name' and 'E-mail' labels. Rename the boxes 'Last_Name' and 'Email'.

Next we need to add a form field for the age range. Although we could use a text field and get the user to type in their age, we don't need to be that exact. All we need to know is whether the user is under 18 or 18 and over. For this, we can use a radio button.

To add a radio button

1 On the Form toolbar, click ⊙ **Radio Button**.

2 Move the cursor next to the 'Age' label and click and drag to insert the radio button. (If you press **Shift** while dragging, the aspect ratio will be maintained.)

3 On the **Transform** tab, set the width and height to 0.7 cm.

To insert a second button, we can copy the first.

4 Press and hold the **Ctrl** key while clicking on the first button and drag it to the right. An exact copy is created.

> 📌 **Radio button properties**
>
> Radio buttons have special properties that include the Field Group. This allows buttons that belong to the same group to work in a mutually exclusive way, ie. only one button can be selected at a time.
>
> For more information about this and other radio button properties, see online Help or the screen tutorial, *Creating a PDF Expenses Form*.

5 Release the **Ctrl** key and position the button in line with the first with a grid column between the two.

6 Right-click the first radio button and then click **Form Field Properties**.

7 In the dialog, in the **Name** text box, type 'Under_18'. Click **OK**.

8 Right-click the second radio button and then click **Form Field Properties**.

9 In the dialog, in the **Name** text box, type '18+'. Click **OK**.

The default properties of the radio buttons will suit our needs for this simple form. However, we do need labels to tell the user what the buttons are for!

10 Click the 📰 **Standard Text Frame** tool and click and drag on the page to place a text frame next to the first radio button.

11 On the Text context toolbar, select the **Body Text Normal** style and type 'Under 18'.

12 Repeat steps 10 and 11 to add a label for '18 and over'.

Our next step is to add a form field for 'Gender.' As there are only ever two options for this, we can use a combo box.

To create a combo box

1 On the Form toolbar, click the 🔽 **Combo Box** button.

2 Move the cursor next to the 'Gender' label. Click and drag on the page to place the combo box.

Now we need to set the properties.

3 Right-click the combo box and then click **Form Field Properties**.

4 In the dialog:

- On the **General** tab, in the **Name** text box type 'Gender'.

- Click the **Options** tab.

- In the **Item** box, type 'Male' and click **Add**. 'Male' appears in the **Item list** box.

- Repeat this process to add 'Female' to the list.

- Click **OK**.

The combo box is now complete. We need to add one more form field to our form—a check box.

To add a check box

1 On the Form toolbar, click the ☒ **Check Box** button.

2 Move the cursor next to the 'special offers' label and click once to add the check box.

3 Right-click the newly placed check box and then click **Form Field Properties**.

4 In the dialog:

- On the **General** tab, in the **Name** text box type 'offers'.

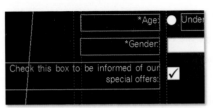

- Click the **Options** tab and select **Checked by default**.

- Click **OK**.

Our form objects are complete. However, before we can publish the form we need to add a **Submit Button** to allow the users to send the data to us.

PDF forms are only useful when you can collect the data. A good way to use this is to use the **Submit Button**. When the user clicks the button, the data is sent to either Serif Web Resources or to your own Web server. Setting this up is easy thanks to the **Form Submit Wizard**.

To use Serif Web Resources, you will need to set up an account. For more information on form data collection, see the topic *Collecting data from forms* in online Help.

To add a Submit Button

1   On the Form toolbar, in the button flyout, click the **Submit Button**.

2   In the Form Submit Wizard:

   • Click **Next** to begin.

   • Click **Next** to use Serif Web Resources.

   • Type a Form ID or click the **Get a Form ID** button, then click **Next**.

   • Leave the **Data format** set to **html** and click **Next**.

   • Click **Finish**.

3   Click and drag on the page beneath the check box to place the button between the layout guides.

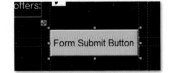

   Let's give the button a useful name.

4   Right-click the button and then click **Form Field Properties**.

5   In the dialog:

   • On the **General** tab, change the **Name** to 'Subscribe_btn'.

   • On the **Options** tab, in the **Caption** box type 'Subscribe'.

   • Click **OK**.

The button text is updated on the page.

That's it, your form is complete! To check your form you'll need to publish it to PDF (it's also a good idea to save your form if you haven't done so already). Let's look at this now.

You can export any PagePlus publication as a PDF file—not just forms. This project covers the basic steps and options. For more information, see *Exporting PDF files* in online Help.

To publish a PDF form

1   On the Standard toolbar, click
     **Publish as PDF**.

2   On the **General** tab, in the **Compatibility** drop-down list, select the appropriate Acrobat version.

3   Select the **Preview PDF File** check box, and then click **OK**.

4   In the **Publish to PDF** dialog, type a file name for the PDF, and save it in a convenient location.

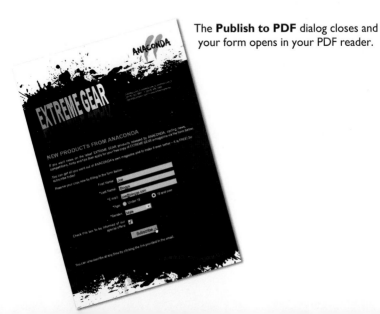

The **Publish to PDF** dialog closes and your form opens in your PDF reader.

Now that you've finished your form, the final step is to create a link to it from a web page and upload it to your website. For more information on this and other web publishing features in PagePlus, see the section, *Producing web pages* in online Help.

Your work is not finished yet—you still need to check your form to make sure that it works in the way you expect.

When checking your form, you should:

- Hover over the form fields and make sure that any ToolTips are spelled correctly.

- Make sure you can type into all text fields.

- Check that all fields are long enough to hold the typed text or predefined list item.

- Check the entries in the combo box drop-down lists—are the items spelled correctly, does all of the text display properly?

- Make sure that you can't select more than one radio button in a group.

Sales Flyer

Whether you're selling your car, organizing an event, or opening a new business, a flyer is an easy to produce, inexpensive, yet effective marketing tool.

In this exercise, you'll learn how to:

- Apply text formatting and adjust text leading.
- Use the **Styles** tab to apply a shadow filter effect.
- Import, position, resize, and crop images.
- Adjust image brightness and contrast.
- Create and position QuickShapes.
- Adjust line and border properties.
- Apply a transparency effect to a shape.

> 🔎 You can use your own images or the sample images provided in the **...\Workspace\Sales Flyer** folder.
>
> In a standard installation, you'll find this folder in the following location:
>
> **C:\Program Files\Serif\PagePlus\X4\Tutorials**

Sales Flyer

In this project, we'll assume that you're selling your car from home, and that you'll be printing your flyer on A4 or Letter sized paper, on a home printer. If you want to use your own images, they should be clear and should show the car from different angles.

Starting with a blank A4 pr Letter document, we'll insert a standard text frame, type a headline, apply some basic text formatting, and create a drop shadow filter effect.

We want our heading to grab the reader's attention, so we need to make it large and bold. You can use any font style you like, but it's generally best to use a sans serif font for headings.

To create a heading using artistic text

1 On the Tools toolbar, click the A ▾ **Artistic Text Tool**, click in the top left corner of the page and type 'FOR SALE'.

2 Triple-click the text object to select both words (or press **Ctrl+A**).

3 On the **Text** context toolbar, choose the font size and style for your heading.

> Normal ▾ Basic Sans Heavy SF ▾ 160 pt ▾

FOR SALE

4 Click between the words for an insertion point, and then press the **Enter** key to place each on a separate line.

Next, we'll adjust the leading—the distance from one line of text to the next.

> You can use the **Fonts** tab to view your currently installed fonts and apply them to your text objects.
>
> Select your text, then hover over a listed font for an in-place preview—if you like what you see, simply click to apply the font to your text.
>
> The tab also hosts a **quick search** feature to filter fonts by name, attribute, or type.

To adjust text leading

- Select the text, then on the **Character** tab, change the leading value to 70%.

Our headline words now sit snugly one on top of the other.

PagePlus provides a variety of filter effects, which you can use to transform any object. We can make our headline text stand out even more by applying a diffused shadow.

To apply a drop shadow

1 Select the text frame.

2 On the **Styles** tab, in the drop-down category list, select **Shadows**.

3 Select an appropriate drop shadow from the **Drop Shadow** sub-category.

4 Click on the thumbnail to apply the effect.

> 📌 The **Styles** tab provides predefined styles that you can apply to objects, or customize to suit your own taste. Each object style can include settings for multiple attributes such as line colour, line style, fill, transparency, filter effects, font, and border. See *Using object styles* in online Help.

Now for the photographs of the car. We'll use four different images for this flyer. They'll need some adjustment though. In these next steps, we'll be resizing, cropping, and adjusting brightness and contrast levels.

To import and resize an image

1 Click outside the text frame to deselect it. On the Tools toolbar, click 🖼 ▾ **Import Picture**.

2 In the **Import Picture** dialog, browse to the ...**Workspace\Sales Flyer** folder and open the **CFSfront.png** file.

3 When the cursor changes to , click and drag on the page to insert the image. (Note that the Picture context toolbar displays.)

4 Resize and move the image until it fits into the space to the right of the headline.

Notice that this image is a little dark. We'll use the Picture context toolbar to adjust it.

To adjust image brightness and contrast

1 Select the image and the Picture context toolbar displays.

2 To adjust brightness, click:

- to increase brightness.

- to decrease brightness.

3 To adjust contrast, click:

- to increase contrast.

- to decrease contrast.

> The **Photo Optimizer** helps you improve the print quality of an image on a specific printer. You can print test samples and choose the best brightness and contrast settings.
>
> With the image selected, on the **Format** menu, click **Picture > Photo Optimizer**, and then follow the instructions in the Wizard.

We'll now insert the main photo for our flyer. We could use the image just as it is. However, there's a lot of background and we're only interested in the car. Let's crop the image, and focus on the car.

To crop an image

1 Repeat steps 1 to 3 of the *To import and resize an image* section to import the **CFSside2.png** file. Resize this image so that it sits beneath the headline and fills the width of the page.

2 With the image selected, on the Attributes toolbar, click the ⊐ **Square Crop Tool**.

3 Click the handle in the upper centre of the image and drag down until you have cropped most of the background.

Repeat the process to crop the background on either side of the car.

4 Repeat steps 1 to 3 of the *To import and resize an image* section to import the **CFSscenery.png** and **CFSside.png** files. Resize these images and position them in the lower right corner of the page, as illustrated.

Great, our images are now in place. They show the car from different angles and give the reader a good idea of its appearance and condition. We'll now insert some text frames and add the car's details and key selling points.

💡 **To fine-tune your cropped image:**

Click in the image (the cursor changes to), and then drag to reposition the image inside the crop boundary. To restore the cropped object to its original shape, click **Remove Crop** on the Crop flyout.

💡 When working with multiple images, instead of importing them one at a time, why not add them all to the **Media Bar**. As you work on your document, you can then quickly view your images and drag and drop them onto the page when you need them. You'll find more details in the **How To** tab and in online Help.

Adding sales text

1 Click the  **Standard Text Frame** tool and insert some text frames in the space at the lower left of the page.

2 Click inside the frames for an insertion point, and then type the car details into the boxes.

   You could use just one text frame. We used three, however, to give us more flexibility with positioning—try dragging the frames around the page to experiment with different positions.

Now for the finishing touches. For a fun effect, we'll use a **QuickShape** and a transparency effect to create pieces of sticky tape to 'stick' our main photo to the page.

To create and format a Quick Shape

1 On the Tools toolbar, on the **QuickShape** flyout, select the **Quick Rectangle**.

2 Click and drag to create a rectangle about 2 x 0.75 cm.

3 On the **Line** tab, set the line weight to **0.5** pt.

4 On the **Colour** tab, click the  **Line** button. Select **Tinting** from the drop-down menu and set the Tint slider to **50**.

We're halfway there—we've created our basic rectangle and lightened its border. To resemble tape, however, our shape has to be transparent.

To add transparency to an object

1   Select the rectangle object.

2   On the **Transparency** tab, click the **Solid** button.

3   Click the **40% Solid Transparency** to apply it to the shape.

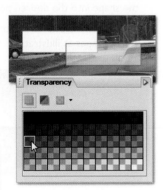

💡 Transparency effects are great for highlights, shading and shadows, and simulating 'rendered' realism. They can make the critical difference between flat-looking illustrations and images with depth and snap.

Now that we've created the template for our 'tape,' we can copy and paste it to quickly create another three identical shapes.

To copy and paste an object

1   Select the object, right-click, and then click **Copy**.

2   Right-click again and click **Paste**.

3   Repeat step 2 twice more to create a total of four identical shapes. The copies will be pasted one on top of the other in the centre of the workspace.

Now all we have to do is position our shapes—we want them to appear to be holding down the corners of our main image. To do this, we need to rotate them.

To rotate an object

1   Click to select the object, hover next to one of the handles —the pointer changes to the **Rotate** cursor—and then drag to rotate the shape.

2   Now click in the centre of the object—the pointer changes to the **Move** cursor—and drag the shape into the desired position.

3   Repeat steps 1 to 3 to rotate and position each of the shapes as illustrated.

That's it! You have successfully created a sales flyer from scratch!

You should now be feeling more familiar with some of PagePlus's powerful desktop publishing tools and features. We hope that you have enjoyed the tutorial!

💡 **Previewing and Printing**

Don't forget that you can preview your document before printing. This is a good habit to get into as it helps you to spot potential problems on the page without wasting ink and paper.

PagePlus supports scaling, tiling, colour separations, and many other useful printing options. For more information, see the *Printing Your Publication* section in online Help.

📌 The PagePlus Page design templates include a selection of ready-made flyer publications, which you can customize to suit your needs.

Address Labels

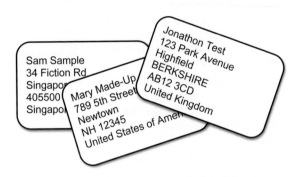

Use PagePlus Mail Merge features to import a simple address list and create mailing labels.

In this project, you'll learn how to:

- Use an Avery label template.
- Open and view a data source.
- Add database records to your page.
- Set up printing options.

Address Labels

In PagePlus, **mail merge** means printing your publication a number of times, inserting different information each time from a data source—in this case an address list file—into a series of form letters or mailing labels.

1   From the Startup Wizard, choose
     Start New Publication and browse
     the **Small Publications > Avery >
     Address Labels** category of blank
     documents.

     Depending on whether you chose a
     US or European setup at the time of
     installation, you'll find either US or
     European label definitions due to the
     differing paper size standards.

> PagePlus can handle many
> kinds of data sources and more
> challenging creative tasks. It's
> even possible to merge picture
> data into single fields or even
> auto-create a grid layout of
> pictures and text suitable for
> catalogues or photo albums (for
> details, see the *Auction Catalogue*
> screen tutorial).

2   Choose either **Parcel L7165** (based
     on A4 paper) or **Namebadge 5095**
     (based on Letter paper) and click **OK**.
     Your publication displays as a single
     label.

3   On the Tools toolbar, click the
     📄 **Standard Text Frame** tool and
     create a text frame to cover the size
     of the page area contained within the
     blue guidelines—if you can't see the
     guidelines, click **View** then
     Guidelines.

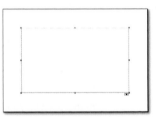

4   On the **Tools** menu, point to **Mail and Photo Merge**, and then
     click **Open Data Source...**.

5   In the **Open** dialog, in the
     Files of Type list
     (highlighted in red in our
     illustration) and select
     **Text Files (*.txt, *.csv,
     *.tab, *.asc)**.

testdata.csv is a comma separated file—entries are delimited by commas—and was created using an address book from an email client program. Most address-management applications and database and spreadsheet programs can create such standard comma-separated files, which you can import.

You can also take advantage of the **New Data Source** command to create your own editable databases in PagePlus.

Select the **testdata.csv** file found in your **Workspace** folder (normally located at:

C:\Program Files\Serif\PagePlus\X4\Tutorials) and click **Open**.

The process of importing your data will begin.

6   In the **Data Format** dialog:

- Click **Delimited**, select **First Line Contains Column Headers**, and then click **Next**.

- Select **Comma**, and then click **Finish**.

The **testdata.csv** file opens and is now your active **data source**. The **Merge List** dialog shows you the active data source and lets you further select, filter, or sort it for the impending merge operation.

For example, you could prevent certain records from being merged, either by clearing the boxes one by one or by applying a filter (for instance, where 'City' is 'Not equal to' 'Nottingham').

7   For now, simply click **OK** to include all the data in your merge list.

You should see the **Mail and Photo Merge** toolbar, indicating that there's an active data source.

8   On the **Mail and Photo Merge** toolbar, click the **Insert Text Field** button.

In the **Insert Text Field** dialog:

- Select **First Name**, click **Insert**, and then press the spacebar.

- Select **Last Name** and click **Insert**.

This inserts the **First Name** and **Last Name** data fields on the same line in your text frame with a space between them.

Now for the address.

9   Press the **Enter** key, select the **Address Line 1** field, click **Insert**, then press the **Enter** key again.

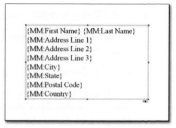

10 Repeat this process of selecting the field name, clicking **Insert**, and then pressing **Enter** until you have inserted each of the address fields on a line of its own in your text frame. Click **Close** when you've finished.

11 On the Frame context toolbar, click the ⊠ **AutoFit** button to force the text to fill the available frame area.

(You can reformat these fields in your text frame as if they were normal text, except that each field will be treated as a single character.)

All of the hard work is done! PagePlus has created the database from an external file and has set up a text frame to contain all of the mail merge data.

12 On the **Mail and Photo Merge** toolbar, click the ▦ **View Data** button. You can now use the arrow buttons on the toolbar (such as the ▶ **Next Record** button) to browse each of the database records in turn merged into your frame.

13 When you're happy to proceed, click the 🖶 **Print** button on the **Standard** toolbar.

14 In the **Print** dialog, click the **Layout** tab.

- In the **Multiple Pages per Sheet** section, on the drop-down menu, choose **Each page N times**. In the **N times** box, set the value to '1.'

- In the **Mail & Photo Merge** section, select the **All records** option.

- Click **Print**.

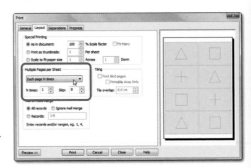

You should now have a printed page containing addresses formatted as if they were on the label you chose at the beginning of the project.

If your address database had consisted of more than eight records, the printed output would have continued on to subsequent pages.

> For instructions on how to print on partially-used label sheets, and how to select which addresses to print, see the *Using mail merge* and *Printing special formats* online Help topics.

Congratulations on successfully creating a mail-merged publication! The same principles can be used to create tailored newsletters, photo-based catalogue layouts, and much more!

Design Packs

Introduction

PagePlus provides a selection of **Design Pack** templates that you can use as starting points for your own publications.

Available from the **Program CD** and **Resource DVD**, these template sets provide a wide range of document types. The following categories may be included in each 'themed' pack:

- Brochures
- Business Cards
- Compliment Slips
- Emails
- Envelopes (C4, C5, DL)
- Flyers
- Letterheads
- Logos
- Menus
- Newsletters
- Posters
- Web Sites

To open a Design Pack template:

1 In the **Startup Wizard**, click **Create > Use Design Template**.

2 In the **Choose a Design Template** dialog, click **Design Packs**, and then browse to and select the template you want to use.

3 Click **OK**.

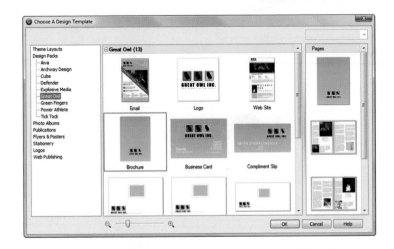

The following pages provide previews of the **Design Pack** templates available on the **PagePlus X4 Program CD** and **Resource DVD**.

💡 For more information about **Design Templates**, see *Creating a publication from a design template* in online Help.

Logo

Front Cover

Inside Spread

Brochure

Back Cover

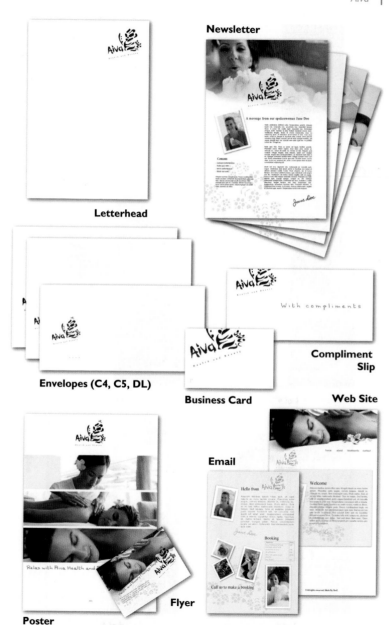

Newsletter

Letterhead

Envelopes (C4, C5, DL)

Business Card

Compliment Slip

Web Site

Poster

Email

Flyer

Logo

Newsletter

1 of 4

2 of 4

3 of 4

4 of 4

Posters

Web Site

Email

Logo

Front Cover

Inside Spread

Brochure

Back Cover

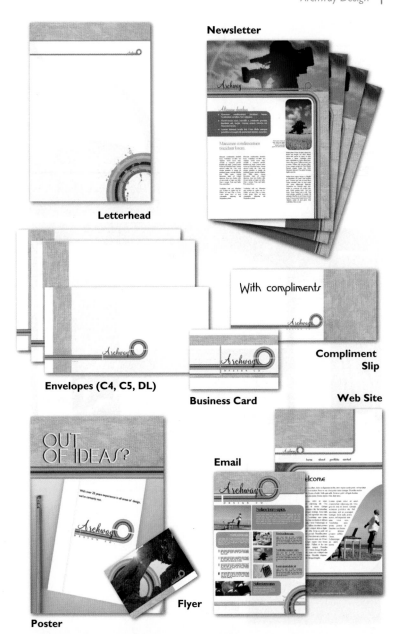

Newsletter

Letterhead

Envelopes (C4, C5, DL)

With compliments

Compliment Slip

Business Card

Web Site

OUT OF IDEAS?

Email

Poster

Flyer

Logo

Front Cover

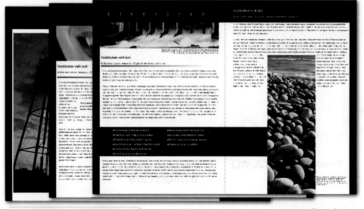

Inside Spread

Brochure

Back Cover

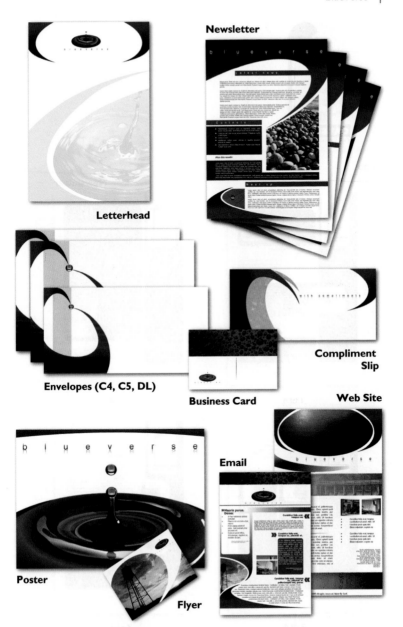

Newsletter

Letterhead

Envelopes (C4, C5, DL)

Business Card

Compliment Slip

Web Site

Email

Poster

Flyer

Logo

Newsletter

1 of 4

2 of 4

3 of 4

4 of 4

Poster

Web Site

Email

Logo

Front Cover

Inside Spread

Brochure

Back Cover

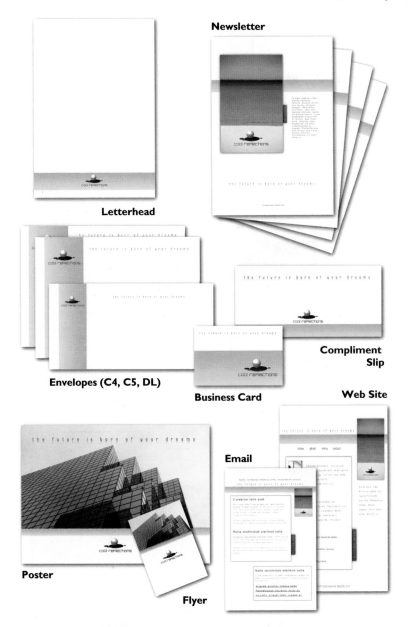

Newsletter

Letterhead

Envelopes (C4, C5, DL)

Business Card

Compliment Slip

Web Site

Email

Poster

Flyer

Logo

Menu

Front

Inside

Back

Inside Back

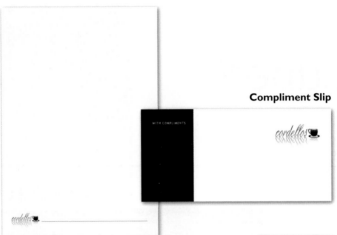

Compliment Slip

Letterhead

Business Card

Poster

Logo

Front Cover

Inside Spread

Brochure

Back Cover

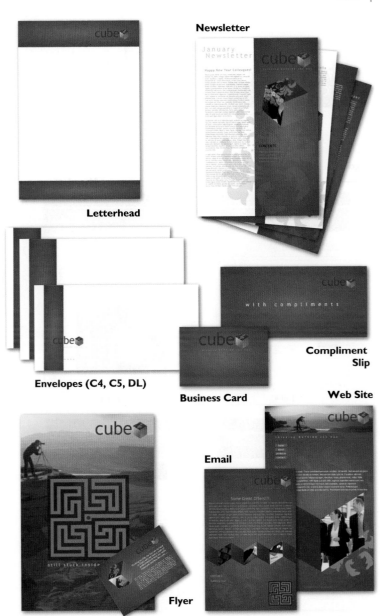

Newsletter

Letterhead

Envelopes (C4, C5, DL)

Business Card

Compliment Slip

Web Site

Email

Poster

Flyer

Logo

Newsletter

1 of 4

2 of 4

3 of 4

4 of 4

Poster

Web Site

Email

Logo

Front Cover

Inside Spread

Brochure

Back Cover

Newsletter

Letterhead

Envelopes (C4, C5, DL)

Compliment Slip

Business Card

Web Site

Email

Poster

Flyer

Logo

Front Cover

Inside Spread

Brochure

Back Cover

Letterhead

Newsletter

Envelopes (C4, C5, DL)

Business Card

Compliment Slip

Web Site

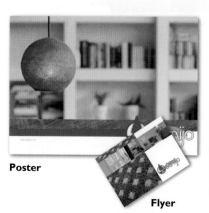

Poster

Flyer

Email

Logo

Front Cover

Inside Spread

Brochure

Back Cover

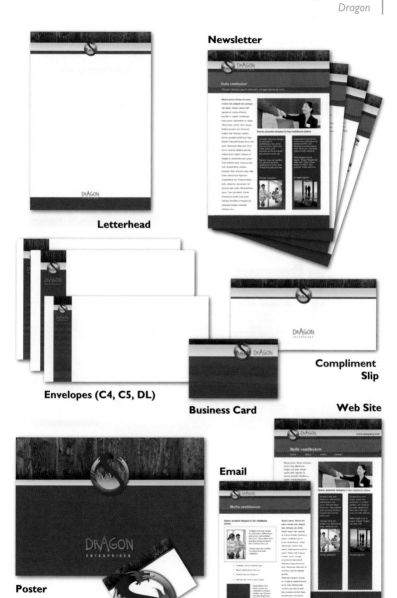

Newsletter

Letterhead

Envelopes (C4, C5, DL)

Business Card

Compliment Slip

Web Site

Email

Poster

Flyer

Logo

Front Cover

Inside Spread

Brochure

Back Cover

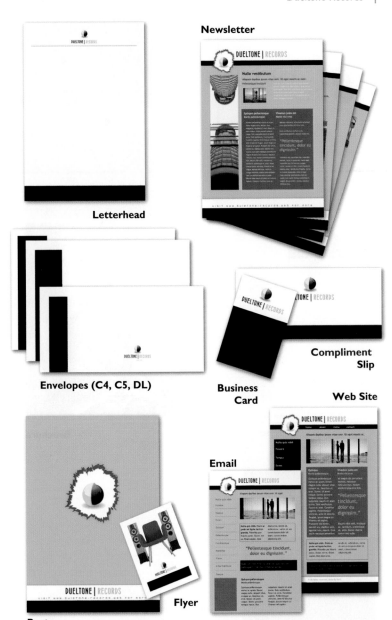

Newsletter

Letterhead

Envelopes (C4, C5, DL)

Business Card

Compliment Slip

Web Site

Email

Poster

Flyer

Logo

Front Cover

Inside Spread

Brochure

Back Cover

Newsletter

Letterhead

Envelopes (C4, C5, DL)

Business Card

Compliment Slip

Web Site

Email

Posters

Flyer

Logo

Front Cover

Inside Spread

Brochure

Back Cover

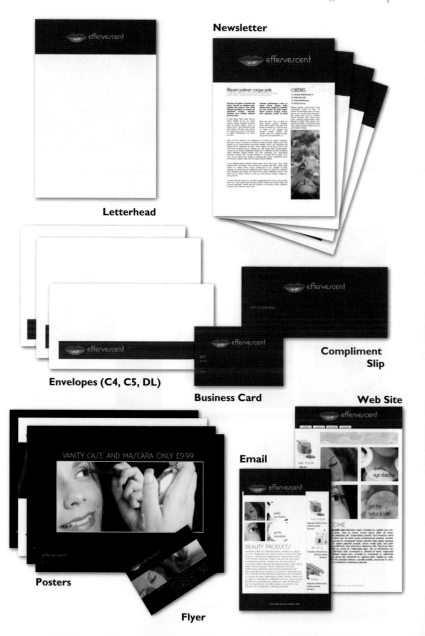

Newsletter

Letterhead

Envelopes (C4, C5, DL)

Business Card

Compliment Slip

Web Site

Email

Posters

VANITY CASE AND MASCARA ONLY £9.99

Flyer

BEAUTY PRODUCTS

Logo

Front Cover

Inside Spread

Brochure

Back Cover

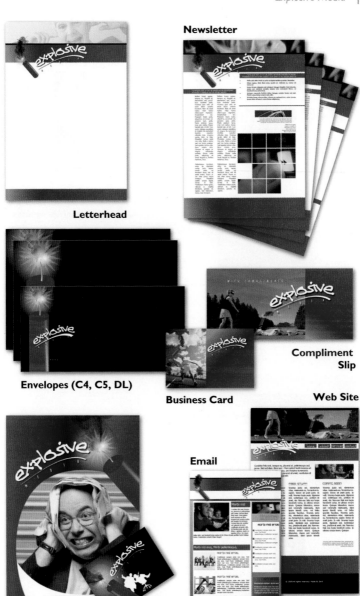

Newsletter

Letterhead

Envelopes (C4, C5, DL)

Compliment Slip

Business Card

Web Site

Email

Poster

Flyer

Logo

Front Cover

Inside Spread

Brochure

Back Cover

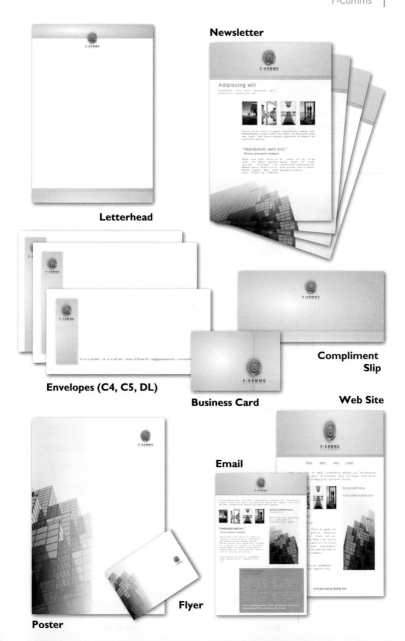

Newsletter

Letterhead

Envelopes (C4, C5, DL)

Compliment Slip

Business Card

Web Site

Email

Poster

Flyer

Logo

Menu

Front

Inside

Back

Inside Back

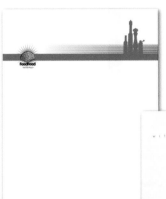

Compliment Slip

Letterhead

Business Card

Web Site

Poster

Logo

Front Cover

Inside Spread

Brochure

Back Cover

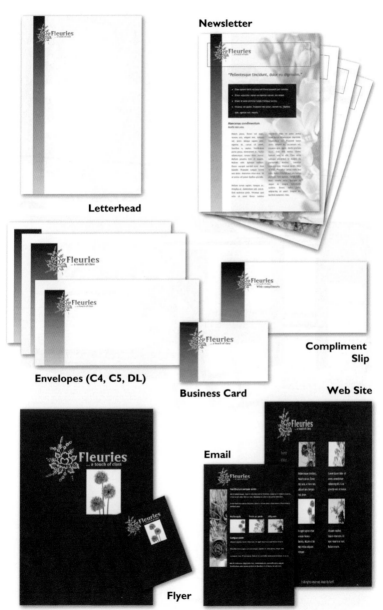

Newsletter

Letterhead

Envelopes (C4, C5, DL)

Business Card

Compliment Slip

Web Site

Email

Poster

Flyer

Logo

Front Cover

Inside Spread

Brochure

Back Cover

Letterhead

Newsletter

Envelopes (C4, C5, DL)

Business Card

Compliment Slip

Web Site

Email

Poster

Flyer

Logo

Front Cover

Inside Spread

Brochure

Back Cover

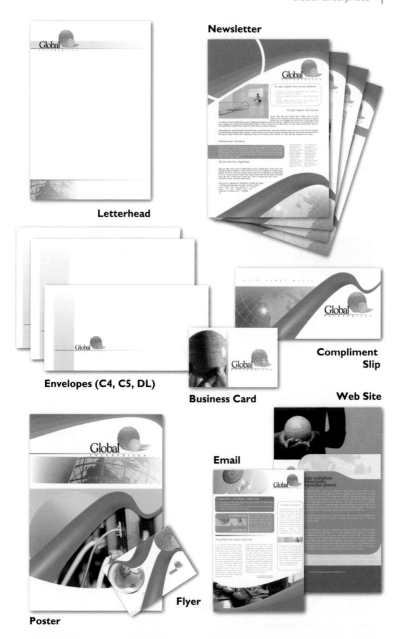

Newsletter

Letterhead

Envelopes (C4, C5, DL)

Business Card

Compliment Slip

Web Site

Email

Poster

Flyer

Logo

Front Cover

Inside Spread

Brochure

Back Cover

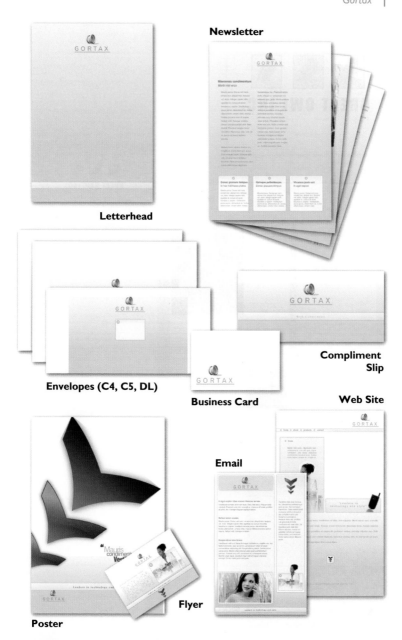

Newsletter

Letterhead

Envelopes (C4, C5, DL)

Business Card

Compliment Slip

Web Site

Email

Poster

Flyer

Logo

Front Cover

Inside Spread

Brochure

Back Cover

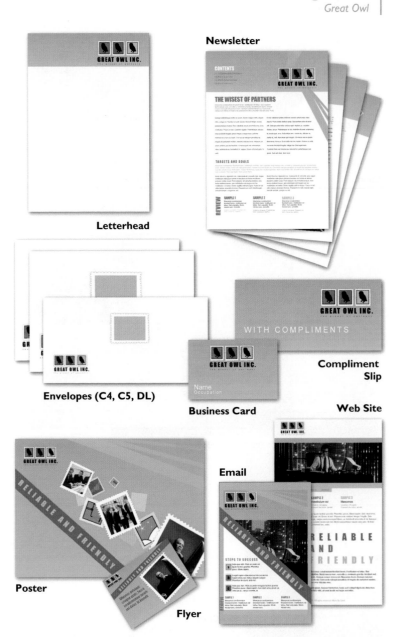

Newsletter

Letterhead

Envelopes (C4, C5, DL)

Business Card

Compliment Slip

Web Site

Poster

Email

Flyer

Logo

Front Cover

Inside Spread

Brochure

Back Cover

Newsletter

Year of the Garden

Contents

Letterhead

Envelopes (C4, C5, DL)

With Compliments

Compliment Slip

Business Card

Web Site

Email

First 100 to join will get a free Gardening guide filled with handy tips!

Get your free book Today!

Posters

Flyer

Logo

Front Cover

Inside Spread

Brochure

Back Cover

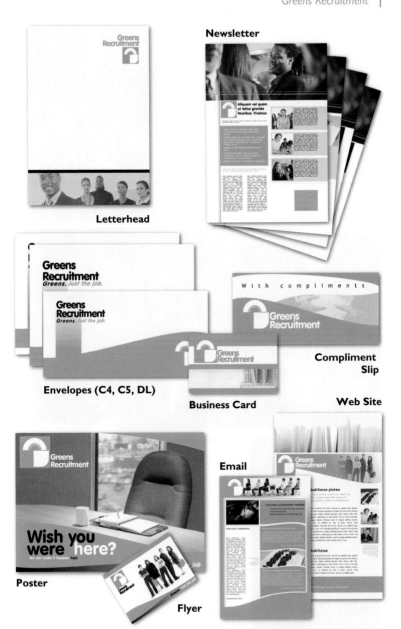

Letterhead

Newsletter

Envelopes (C4, C5, DL)

Business Card

Compliment Slip

Web Site

Poster

Email

Flyer

Greens
Recruitment
Greens. Just the job.

With compliments

Wish you
were here?
We can make it happen. Fast.

Logo

Front Cover

Inside Spread

Brochure

Back Cover

Newsletter

Letterhead

Envelopes (C4, C5, DL)

Compliment Slip

Business Card

Web Site

Email

Poster

Flyer

Logo

Front Cover

Inside Spread

Brochure

Back Cover

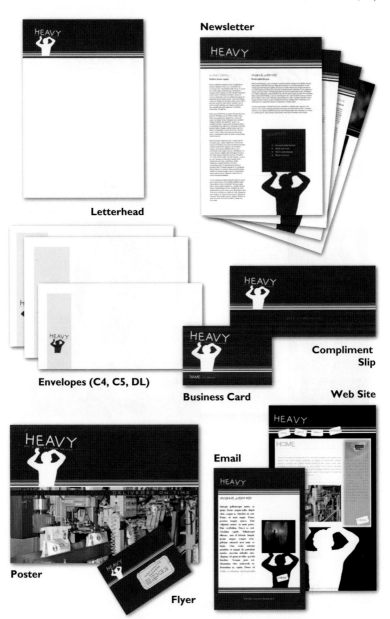

Newsletter

Letterhead

Envelopes (C4, C5, DL)

Business Card

Compliment Slip

Web Site

Poster

Email

Flyer

Logo

Front Cover

Inside Spread

Brochure

Back Cover

Newsletter

Letterhead

Envelopes (C4, C5, DL)

Compliment Slip

Business Card

Web Site

Email

Poster

Flyer

Logo

Menu

Front

Inside

Back

Inside Back

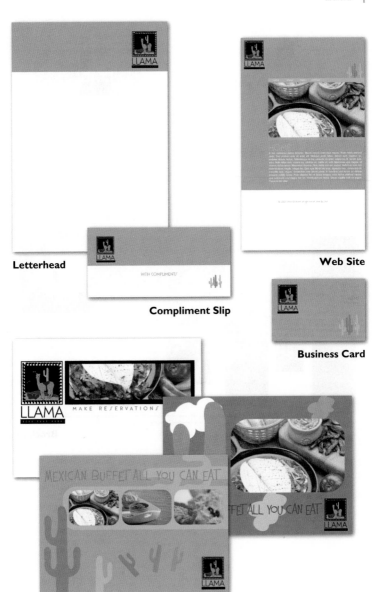

Letterhead

Compliment Slip

Web Site

Business Card

Posters

Logo

Front Cover

Inside Spread

Brochure

Back Cover

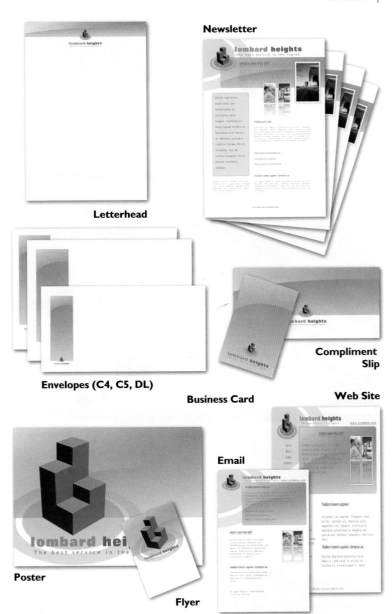

Newsletter

Letterhead

Envelopes (C4, C5, DL)

Compliment Slip

Business Card

Web Site

Email

Poster

Flyer

Logo

Front Cover

Inside Spread

Brochure

Back Cover

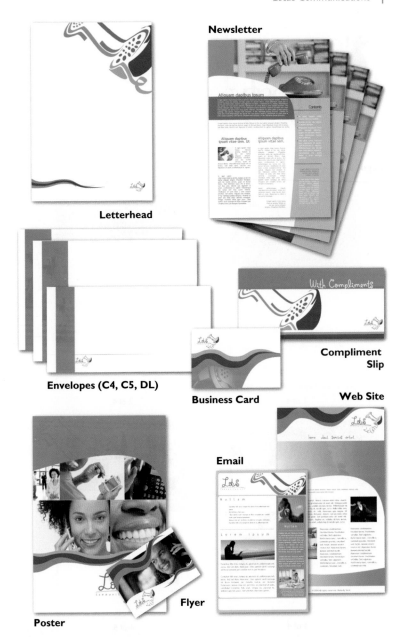

Newsletter

Letterhead

Envelopes (C4, C5, DL)

Business Card

Compliment Slip

Web Site

Email

Poster

Flyer

Logo

Newsletter

1 of 4

2 of 4

3 of 4

4 of 4

Poster

Web Site

Email

Logo

Front Cover

Inside Spread

Brochure

Back Cover

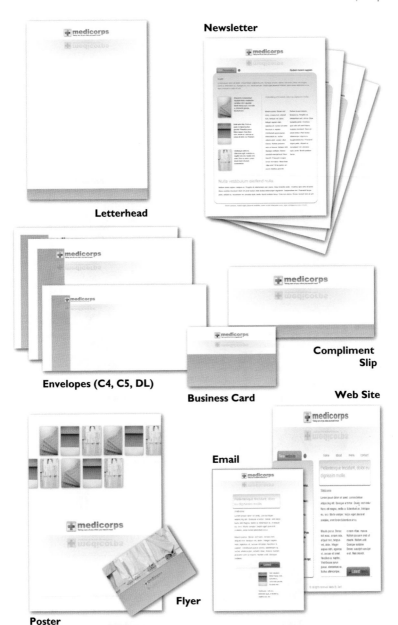

Newsletter

Letterhead

Envelopes (C4, C5, DL)

Business Card

Compliment Slip

Web Site

Email

Poster

Flyer

Logo

Newsletter

1 of 4

2 of 4

3 of 4

4 of 4

Poster

Email

Web Site

Logo

Front Cover

Inside Spread

Brochure

Back Cover

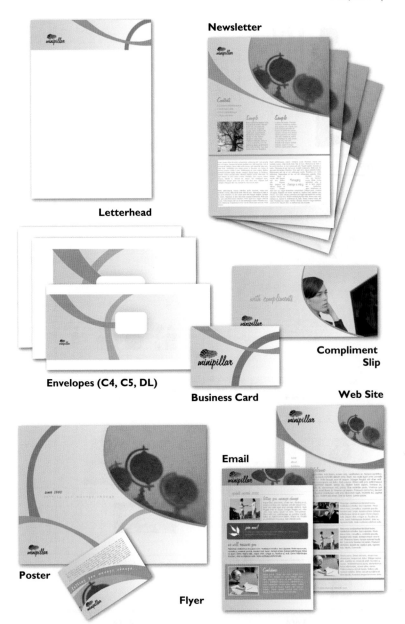

Newsletter

Letterhead

Envelopes (C4, C5, DL)

Business Card

Compliment Slip

Web Site

Poster

Email

Flyer

Logo

Newsletter

1 of 4

2 of 4

3 of 4

4 of 4

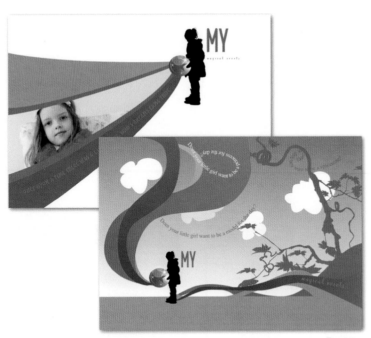

Posters

Email

Web Site

Logo

Menu

Front

Inside

Back

Inside Back

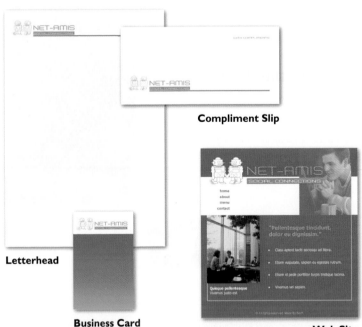

Compliment Slip

Letterhead

Business Card

Web Site

Poster

Logo

Front Cover

Inside Spread

Brochure

Back Cover

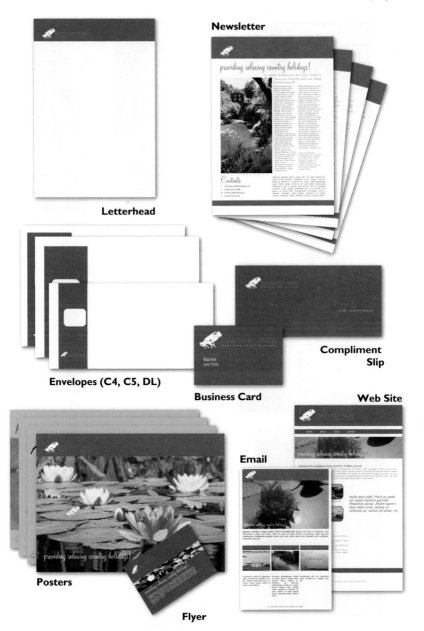

Newsletter

Letterhead

Envelopes (C4, C5, DL)

Business Card

Compliment Slip

Web Site

Posters

Email

Flyer

providing relaxing country holidays!

Logo

Front Cover

Inside Spread

Brochure

Back Cover

Newsletter

Letterhead

Envelopes (C4, C5, DL)

Business Card

Compliment Slip

Web Site

Poster

Email

Flyer

Logo

Front Cover

Inside Spread

Brochure

Back Cover

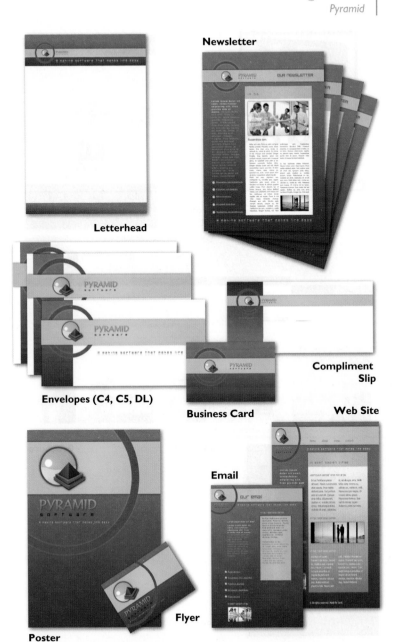

Newsletter

Letterhead

Envelopes (C4, C5, DL)

Business Card

Compliment Slip

Web Site

Email

Poster

Flyer

Logo

Front Cover

Inside Spread

Brochure

Back Cover

Newsletter

Letterhead

Envelopes (C4, C5, DL)

Business Card

Compliment Slip

Web Site

Email

Posters

Flyer

Logo

Newsletter

1 of 4

2 of 4

3 of 4

4 of 4

Posters

Web Site

Email

Logo

Newsletter

1 of 4

2 of 4

3 of 4

4 of 4

Poster

Web Site

Email

Logo

Front Cover

Inside Spread

Brochure

Back Cover

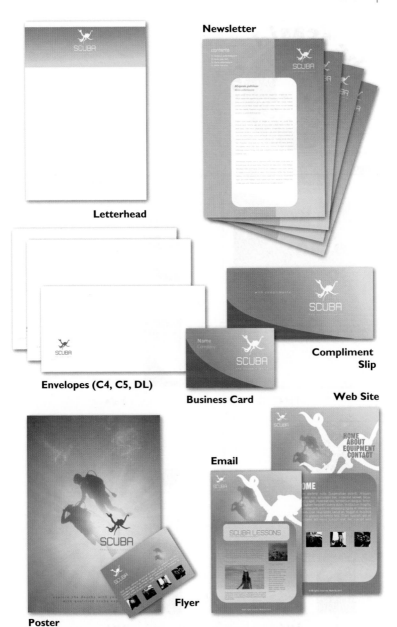

Newsletter

Letterhead

Envelopes (C4, C5, DL)

Business Card

Compliment Slip

Web Site

Email

Poster

Flyer

Logo

Newsletter

1 of 4

2 of 4

3 of 4

4 of 4

Posters

Web Site

Email

Logo

Newsletter

1 of 4

2 of 4

3 of 4

4 of 4

Poster

Web Site

Email

Logo

Front Cover

Inside Spread

Brochure

Back Cover

Newsletter

Letterhead

Envelopes (C4, C5, DL)

Business Card

Compliment Slip

Web Site

Poster

Flyer

Email

Logo

Front Cover

Inside Spread

Brochure

Back Cover

Newsletter

Letterhead

Envelopes (C4, C5, DL)

Business Card

Compliment Slip

Web Site

Email

Poster

Flyer

Logo

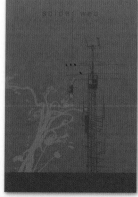

Front Cover

Inside Spread

Brochure

Back Cover

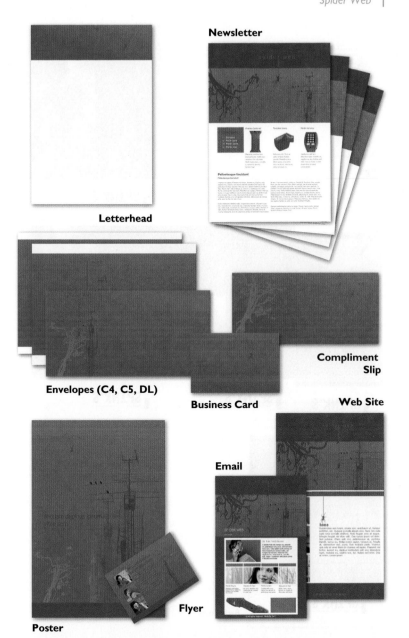

Newsletter

Letterhead

Envelopes (C4, C5, DL)

Business Card

Compliment Slip

Web Site

Email

Poster

Flyer

Logo

Front Cover

Inside Spread

Brochure

Back Cover

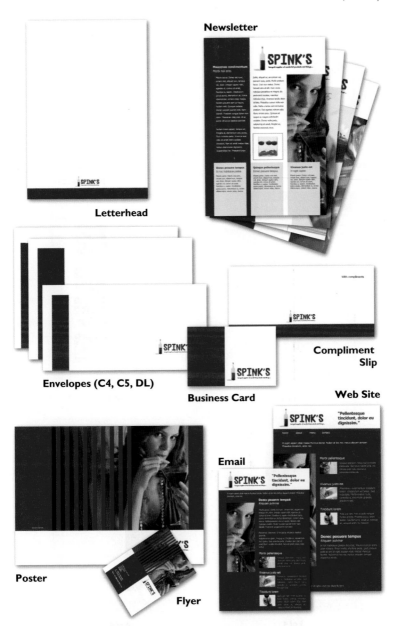

Newsletter

Letterhead

Envelopes (C4, C5, DL)

Business Card

Compliment Slip

Web Site

Email

Poster

Flyer

Logo

Newsletter

1 of 4

2 of 4

3 of 4

4 of 4

Poster

Web Site

Email

Logo

Front Cover

Inside Spread

Brochure

Back Cover

Newsletter

Letterhead

Envelopes (C4, C5, DL)

Business Card

Compliment Slip

Web Site

Email

Poster

Flyer

Logo

1 of 4

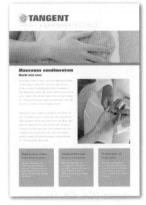

2 of 4

3 of 4

4 of 4

Poster

Web Site

Email

Logo

Front Cover

Inside Spread

Brochure

Back Cover

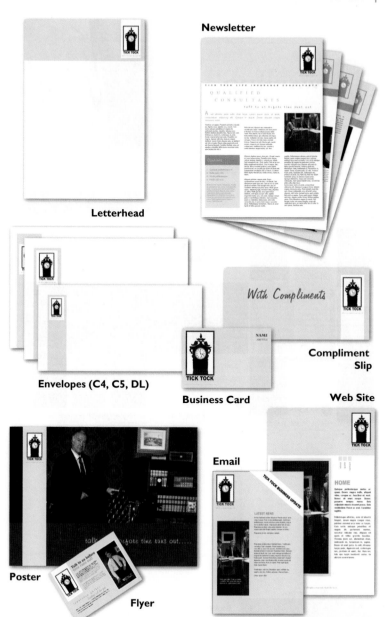

Newsletter

Letterhead

Envelopes (C4, C5, DL)

Business Card

Compliment Slip

Web Site

Email

Poster

Flyer

Logo

Front Cover

Inside Spread

Brochure

Back Cover

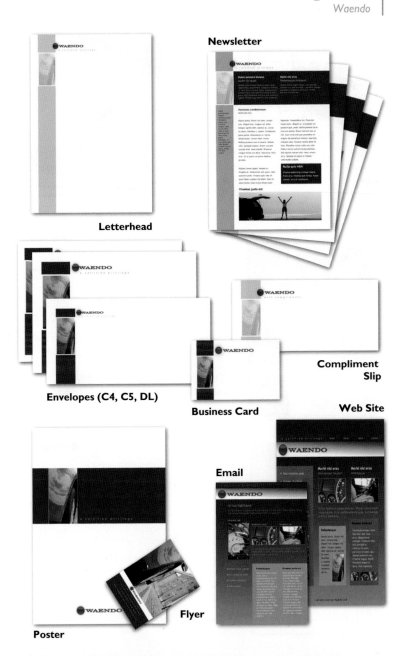

Newsletter

Letterhead

Envelopes (C4, C5, DL)

Compliment Slip

Business Card

Web Site

Email

Poster

Flyer

Logo

Front Cover

Inside Spread

Brochure

Back Cover

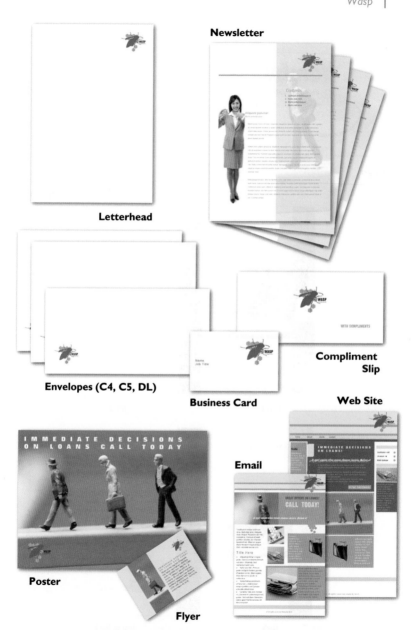

Newsletter

Letterhead

Envelopes (C4, C5, DL)

Business Card

Compliment Slip

Web Site

Poster

Email

Flyer

Logo

Menu

Front

Inside

Back

Inside Back

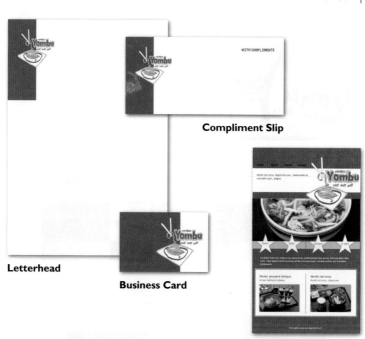

Compliment Slip

Letterhead

Business Card

Web Site

Poster

Logo

Newsletter

1 of 4

2 of 4

3 of 4

4 of 4

Poster

Web Site

Email

Logo

Front Cover

Inside Spread

Brochure

Back Cover

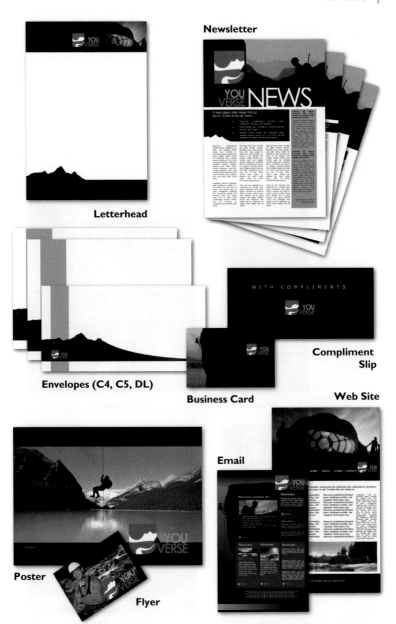

Newsletter

Letterhead

Envelopes (C4, C5, DL)

Business Card

Compliment Slip

Web Site

Email

Poster

Flyer

Logo

Front

Inside

Back

Inside Back

Compliment Slip

Letterhead

Business Card

Poster

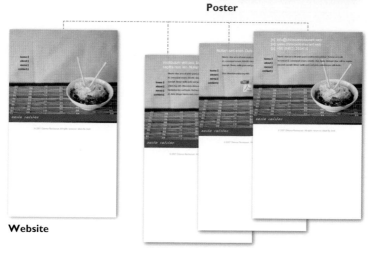

Website

Theme Layouts

Introduction

PagePlus includes a selection of **Theme Layout** templates that you can use as starting points for your own publications.

Available from the **Program CD**, the theme layouts offer a range of layout styles. Each theme includes the following document types:

- Brochure
- Business Card
- Flyer
- Newsletter
- Poster

To open a Theme Layout:

1 In the **Startup Wizard**, click **Create > Use Design Template**.

2 In the **Choose a Design Template** dialog:

- Select **Theme Layouts**.

- Browse to and select the layout you want to use.

- Choose the colour scheme you want to apply from the upper-right drop-down list.

- Select the pages to include in the layout.

- Click **OK**.

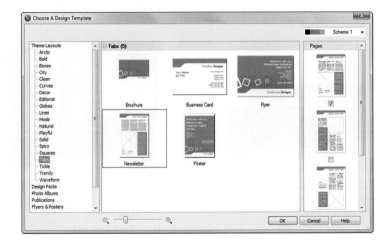

The following pages provide previews of the **Theme Layout** templates included on the **PagePlus X4 Program CD**.

Brochure

Business Card

Flyer

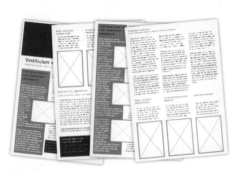

Newsletter

Poster

Brochure

Business Card

Newsletter

Flyer

Poster

Brochure

Business Card

Flyer

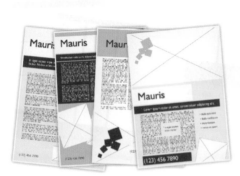

Newsletter

Poster

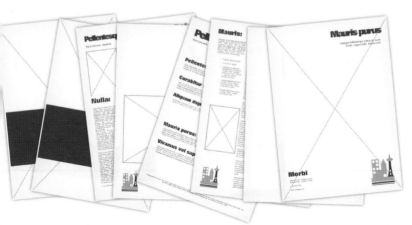

Brochure

Business Card

Flyer

Newsletter

Poster

Brochure

Business Card

Flyer

Newsletter

Poster

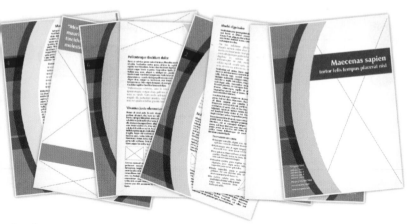

Brochure

Business Card

Flyer

Newsletter

Poster

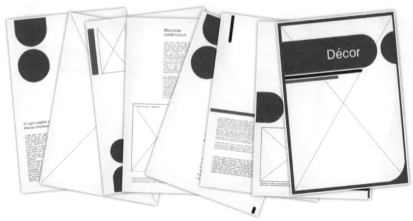

Brochure

Business Card

Flyer

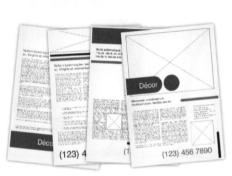

Newsletter

Poster

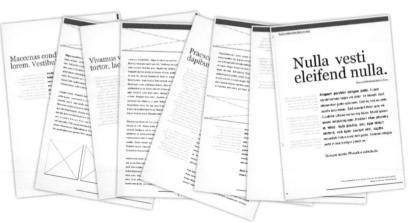

Brochure

Business Card

Flyer

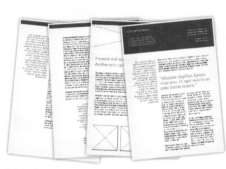

Newsletter

Poster

Brochure

Business Card

Flyer

Newsletter

Poster

Brochure

Business Card

Flyer

Newsletter

Poster

Brochure

Business Card

Flyer

Newsletter

Poster

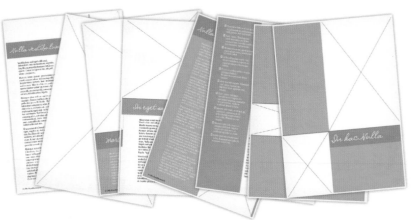

Brochure

Business Card

Flyer

Newsletter

Poster

Brochure

Business Card

Flyer

Newsletter

Poster

Brochure

Business Card

Flyer

Newsletter

Poster

Brochure

Business Card

Flyer

Newsletter

Poster

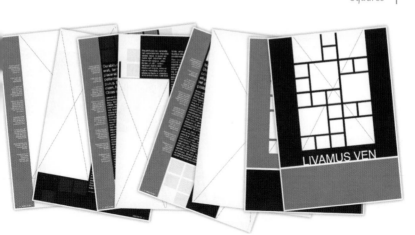

Brochure

Business Card

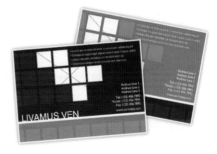

Flyer

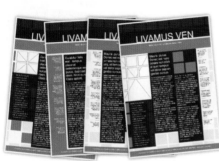

Newsletter

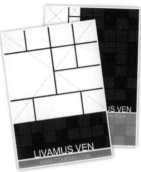

Poster

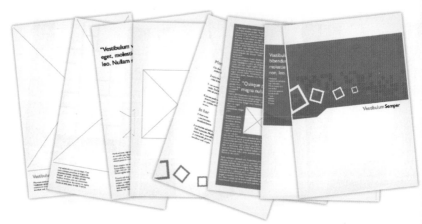

Brochure

Business Card

Flyer

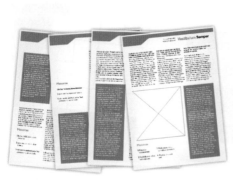

Newsletter

Poster

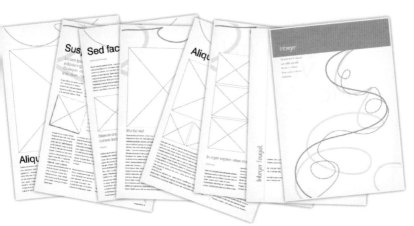

Brochure

Business Card

Flyer

Newsletter

Poster

Brochure

Business Card

Flyer

Newsletter

Poster

Brochure

Business Card

Flyer

Newsletter

Poster

LogoStudio & Logo Templates

Introduction

LogoStudio is a purpose-built environment that lets you create and edit logos in isolation from other page elements. You can create your own logos from scratch, or choose from a range of logo templates.

Transfer of data between LogoStudio and PagePlus is transparent and seamless, and you can jump between the two environments at any time.

The PagePlus X4 Program CD provides a wide selection of logo templates, each offering a choice of layouts and colour sets. You can use the templates 'as is,' or customize them to suit your needs.

The **Insert Logo** dialog also includes a collection of ready-made design elements (Flashes), which you can add to any of your publications.

 Additional logos are available on the PagePlus Resource DVD.

Using LogoStudio

LogoStudio's intuitive user interface focuses on the main tools and techniques you'll need, and provides step-by-step instructions to help you create and refine your logo.

To create a logo from scratch:

1   On the Tools toolbar, click 🖎 **Insert Logo**.

2   In the **Insert Logo** dialog, select the blank thumbnail from the Blank section in the left pane.

3   Click **Open**.

4   Click or click and drag to place the logo on the page. The LogoStudio environment opens automatically.

5   To create your design, you can use the interactive **How To** tab elements, or the traditional PagePlus creation tools.

To edit an existing logo:

1   Click the 🖎 **Edit in LogoStudio** button that displays on the control bar under the selected logo.

    - or -

    On the Tools toolbar, on the Logo flyout, click 🖎 **Edit in LogoStudio**.

    - or -

    Right-click the logo and select **Edit in LogoStudio...**

    LogoStudio opens with your object(s) zoomed in to fit your workspace.

2   To customize your logo design, use the interactive **How To** tab elements, or the traditional PagePlus creation tools.

🔖 For more information on creating logos in LogoStudio, see the LogoStudio **How To** tab and *Creating Logos* in online Help.

To create a logo from an existing template:

1   On the Tools toolbar, click 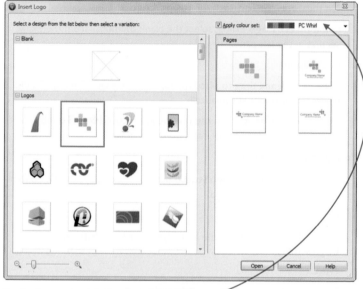 **Insert Logo**.

2   In the **Insert Logo** dialog, select a design template from the **Logos** panel, and then choose your template layout from the **Pages** panel. (These differ depending on the template chosen.)

3   In the upper right corner of the dialog:

    • To apply the colour scheme of the publication, clear the **Apply colour set** check box.

    - or -

    • To apply a colour set, select the **Apply colour set** check box, and then select a colour set from the drop-down list.

4   Click **Open**.

5   **Optional:** If you have chosen a logo containing text objects, the **Customize Your Logo** dialog opens, allowing you to edit the text.

6   Click **OK**.

To insert the logo at default size, click on your page; to set the size of the logo, click and drag out a region and release the mouse button.

Logo Templates

Each template provides a choice of layouts and colour sets. For example, the template on the right offers the layout and colour set options displayed below.

The following pages display all of the logo templates. To see their respective layout and colour set options, you can browse the templates in the **Insert Logo** dialog or from the **Gallery** tab.

Colour Scheme: PC Whirl

Colour Scheme: Lab

Colour Scheme: dot.com